Why I
Hate the
Democrats

Why I Hate the Democrats

RANDY HOWE

The Lyons Press

Guilford, Connecticut
An imprint of The Globe Pequot Press

To Chris Kuebler

The Lyons Press is an imprint of The Globe Pequot Press.

10 9 8 7 6 5 4 3 2 1

Printed in the United States of America

Designed by Heather Kern

ISBN 1-59228-436-1

Library of Congress Cataloging-in-Publication Data is available on file.

Author's Notice

Asinus asinum fricat.

This is a book about politics and politicians, so—fittingly—all manner of spin doctoring, poetic license, and gerrymandering of the truth have been employed.

Caveat emptor.
Caveat Democrat.

Contents

Charity creates a multitude of sins.
—Oscar Wilde

I hate the idea of causes.
—E. M. Forster, from
Two Cheers for Democracy

When they call the roll in the Senate,
the senators do not know whether to
answer "present" or "guilty."
—Theodore Roosevelt,
twenty-sixth President of the
United States, carrying his big stick

You've got to be an optimist to be a
Democrat, and you've got to be a
humorist to stay one.
—Will Rogers

'69 Corvette Convertible

Nature . . . is nothing but the inner voice of
self-interest.
—Charles Baudelaire, in
"The Painter of Modern Life"

What do I think of when I think of the Democrats? Jackasses in glass
houses, throwing sanctimonious stones and wolves in sheep's clothing preaching holier than thou. I might be only an average joe who
nobody knows, but I'm not gullible. I know people. I know myself.
I know politics. And most of all, I know the Democratic Party. Their
history of self-righteous hypocrisy is what has me feeling one step
past peeved. Holier than no one.

Unlike Al Franken and Michael Moore, you've never seen me
before. I talk, but I'm no talk-
ing head: on a daily basis the
listening is done courtesy of my
students. Every morning I
commute forty-five minutes to
teach the difference between

I am easy-going right
up to the borders of
my self-interest.
—Mason Cooley

> I despise the kind of existence that clings to the miserly trifles of comfort and self-interest.
> —Fidel Castro

left and right and right and wrong. At least a half hour of that commute is spent in I-95 traffic; the drive would be so much nicer in a convertible . . .

I'd much rather save my nickels and dimes for the purchase of that convertible—a '69 Stingray is the dream, although I'd settle for a crappy ol' Caddy—than hand it over to some numbskull, let alone a Congress of numbskulls, let alone a Congress of Democratic numbskulls intent on redistributing it. Come April 15th, I see just how much I've done for my fellow man. I'm reminded of how much I'd like to do for my family and for myself. The only thing more personal than needs is wants.

Truth be told, I was a Democrat until my eighteenth birthday, but I registered in the midst of the Dukakis turkey shoot, and Independent just seemed the way to go. Anyone with a grasp of U.S. history knows why, despite my career in education, I continue to deny the donkey. I've had enough of Democrats promising it all and delivering nada. I've found, time and time again, that their bray is far worse than their bite. The Democrats may be symbolized by the *Equus asinus asinus,* but today's party leadership can be divided into two detestable factions, neither of which makes me happy: the docile, bleeding-heart sheep and the conniving, self-serving wolves. The former is philanthropy to a fault, the latter is personal profit to a fault. The donkey sways between the two, pleasing no one but himself.

I may be a nobody, but I take pride in my teaching. I take pride in fulfilling the promise of education. It's amazing, though, to think of all that I could get away with if I behaved like one of those

> Communism doesn't work because people like to own stuff.
> —Frank Zappa

Democratic bigwigs. For example, I could tell an aide to watch my class and to just call me should a principal or parent come around. For all I care, each student could finish the year dumb as a stump, satisfied with their knowledge of video games and cartoons. They'd be as pleased as their parents, to whom I'd simply say those things they want to hear. Promise them the moon and deliver a marble. My days could be filled with recess and the newspaper. A nice, easy life under the guise of helping others.

> Beware of false prophets, who come to you in sheep's clothing but inwardly are ravenous wolves.
> —*The Bible*, Matthew 7:15

And as far as my personal coffers are concerned, I like the idea of charging a "per plate" if colleagues want to eat lunch with me. For a mere $10,000, I'd warm them up with a joke about our rival elementary school, roll up my sleeves for that Howard Dean work-ethic effect, get all sentimental about the special-ed kids, and then bid all of my fellow teachers adieu, pointing as I leave the staff lounge to those who seem the most desperate for recognition. I'd kiss a baby before making my way to another exotic locale—someplace like the bed in the nurse's office. After a nap, I'd commandeer a bus and go tutor, earning my salary at school while moonlighting (cash,

> I've spent the night on a dairy farm here in Wisconsin. If I'm entrusted with the presidency, you'll have someone who is very familiar with what the Wisconsin dairy industry is all about.
> —Al Gore, campaigning unconvincingly in 2000

> Hillary's pretensions to having loved New York all her life are just convenient fabrications . . . Hillary does not want to join us. She will agree to live with us only if we send her to Washington. We are no more than a launching pad. When Hillary poses in a Yankee hat, it turns our stomachs.
>
> —Dick Morris[1]

under the table, of course). If I got caught, I could justify the bus as part of my "outreach program." I'd have to call a reporter for some positive press, too: photos of Little Jimmy and me leaning diligently over a book. Even a blind man could see that I'm a guy who cares. Yes indeedy, feed the needy! Speaking of which, at the end of the day, I'd pilfer some Tater Tots from the cafeteria for my after-school snack. Hey, I deserve it, right? A couple of cartons of chocolate milk to wash the taters down and then out to the 'Vette I'd bought with the money from the PTA bake sale.[2]

In this way, I could be the typical jackass. I could be a Democrat.

I'm tempted. I mean, I could play nice whenever someone is watching and just kick it into high gear when tenure time rolls around. Just like an election year—win, then recede into a state of glorious sloth. Lame duck education.

But no. I'm going to stay the course. I will be the teacher that all kids deserve and I will never, ever rejoin the Democratic ranks. Rather, I will rank on them and their leadership. From the early days

---

[1] Morris had worked as a Clinton political strategist, hired for his insight and cutting commentary . . .

[2] I leave early because the chances of me sticking around for bus duty are about as good as the Pope granting Tom Daschle sainthood.

of the Electoral College to Bill's intern bagging and Hillary's carpet-bagging, to the usual suspects that get rounded up every four years; from Jefferson to JFK to LBJ, all the way up to today, no one is exempt.

I think it's the hypocrisy that bothers me most. Instead of walking the walk, the Democrats continually stop short after talking the talk. I don't really hate anybody—I'm a teacher, after all! That being said, there are things that I truly hate. I hate it when my daughter has a fever. I hate 99.9 percent of reality shows and I hate having to sit through ads before the $9 movie starts. I hate the word congealed. I really hate sitting in traffic and I really, really, really hate that percentage of the Democratic Party that has made a living out of breaking its promises. (Does 99.9 percent ring a bell?) What gets me the most is when children are the promisee and the promiser fails to come through.

On that note, if I see another photo of some jackass candidate reading to kids—last I checked, fifth-graders were well beyond Dr. Seuss!—I might just go postal. Some nasty teacher ninja kung fu will be headed Senator Blowhard's way. They'll have to change the phrase to "go teacher."

> Farmer's Day is bigger. The only difference is we have four-legged jackasses on Farmer's Day and we have two-legged jackasses today.
> —G. A. McCaskill, on the celebration of John Edwards's presidential campaign

The Democratic elite bah and bray, crying out for money and compassion when they themselves are already well stocked in the former and have no intention of showing any of the latter. Public servants with private interests. The candidates like to talk of blue-collar upbringings, even though their parents had plenty of money for college and the like. Someone should tell John Edwards—whose worth was listed at more than $12 million in 2003—that blue collar doesn't mean an Italian dress shirt from Brooks Brothers!

Admittedly, politics is driven by self-interest, and self-interest means keeping enough of what you earn to help the family out; maybe even treat yourself to something nice every now and again (that convertible would sure help my commute . . .). Human nature says I want to keep what's mine and I'll share when I damn well please. The Democrats have yet to figure out a way to alter human nature, but they are still hell-bent on trying.

Still, true walk-the-walk liberals I can live with. I may not vote for them, but I can listen to what they have to say. On the other

> You can't make a silk purse out of a sow's ear, and you can't change human nature from intelligent self-interest into pure idealism—not in this life; and if you could, what would be left for paradise?
> —Congressman Joseph Gurney Cannon (R-IL)

hand, the Land Rover Liberals who currently head the Democratic Party . . . I just don't want to hear it. They're the congealed fat in the bottom of my McDonald's bag as I'm stuck in traffic on the way to pick my sick daughter up from day care (so that we can see a $9 movie!). I need someone I can believe in, someone who means it when he says he's looking out for the average joe, someone who's willing to admit that he has wants like mine and needs like mine, someone honest and effective and inspiring. Someone human.

When I first typed "What do I think of when I think of the Democrats?", things were really starting to heat up in Iraq, and the donkeys were just beginning to wring their worried little hooves over the upcoming election. Memories of 9/11 were still fresh in my mind. I think that the best way to come to terms with loss on such a grand scale is to compartmentalize it, and then to tackle the antecedents and the consequences head-on. No pussyfooting. No kid gloves. It's how the nation needs to address all of the problems of the new millennium, both foreign and domestic. It's what we deserve—yes, *deserve*—from our leaders. Honesty, pure as a child admitting he took another kid's Tater Tots. The truth, like a dodge ball to the head.

Until that kind of sincerity and common sense become trademarks of the Democratic Party, it's open season, and I'm Charlton Heston, Ted Nugent, and Teddy Roosevelt all rolled into one.

I'm about to "go teacher."

> Only a coward supports gun control.
> You know how to stop carjacking? Shoot the
> carjacker. If someone is going to kill me for
> my Buick, I'm gonna shoot until I'm out of
> ammo—and then I'll call 911.
> —Ted Nugent

Why I
Hate the
Democrats

Chapter One

Commonsense Radio Network:
Monday

Always forgive your enemies;
nothing annoys them so much.
—Oscar Wilde

I don't make jokes. I just watch
the government and report the facts.
—Will Rogers

"Good morning, everyboooooody. Respecting the rights of all American citizens and convinced that the cream always rises to the top, this is G. David Hopewell, and you're listening to Radio America! As we do every day from 6:00 to 10:00 A.M., I'm coming to you live from the studios of the Commonsense Radio Network, where the reception's clear and so's the logic. In case you haven't noticed, there's an election on the horizon and, as the economy gains momentum, so, too, do the approval ratings for all Republicans, from governors to representatives to senators to the president. It looks like another clean sweep for the GOP!

"Where there's smoke there's fire, though, and the Democrats are fanning the flames. The use of our troops in the Middle East is still being questioned, and unions are making more noise than ever about free trade agreements. The Oprah Nation is standing at attention, just waiting for their marching orders and, like with that book club of hers, as soon as the endorsement comes—Kerry? Dean? Sharpton? *Hillary?*—off they'll go. Don't! Get! Me! Started!

"Actually, get me started. Please! With so much to talk about, I'm counting on Charlie there behind the glass to connect me with you, the listener. *Buenas dias*, Charlie!"

"Morning, G. Man. Speaking of Spanish, we have a caller for you on line nine. Mexican-born but now a resident of Tempe, Arizona, it's Esteban."

"G! *¿Que pasa?*"

"In the bond of all things red, white, and blue . . . Hit me with some salt and a lime, Esteban!"

> It is difficult to generalize why so many Latino/as moved toward conservative views. For many, I believe it is basically a matter of desiring material acquisitions.
> —Ana Castillo, poet

"Okay. I've just about had it, *jefe*. Am I really supposed to believe my mother worked eighty hours a week to get her kids educated just so I could give thirty percent of my paycheck to the government? *Es* ridiculous, G."

"I know it, *hermano*. Bigger government means bigger taxes. What can you do but fight the good fight?"

"Just so's you know, I'm a legal."

> We own the Hispanic vote.
> —Diane Feinstein, before losing the California
> gubernatorial election to a Republican

"Illegal?"

"No. A *legal!* A legal citizen. I'm mad because my kids go to public school and illegal alien kids go to the same school! They get the same teachers, same books, same pencils, same lunches. Same as *mis hijos* . . . I don't understand how this can be."

"Well, Esteban, the deal is this: We've got to support children. No matter how fiscally sound we want to be, you can't mess with kids. It's not their fault *madre y padre* are illegal aliens, you know? When they grow up, they'll be citizens. Proud citizens, just like you. At least, that's the hope. They'll register for the draft and they'll fight for their country.

"Just so long as they're spending the cash they earn right here in the U.S., spurring on the economy and being productive citizens. Naturalize them and collect some taxes on their earnings, I say. It's when they send all of their money to Latin America that it's time to clamp down."

"*Sí, mi amigo.* I see what you're saying. God bless America and have a good one!"

CLICK.

"*Adios, hombre.* And *gracias*, Charlie. It's nice to hear from an intelligent—that is, someone who agrees with me!—listener every once in a while. The problem is, most of them are at work, so only the nutty, numbskull Democrats can call in. But back to Esteban, it's interesting how the Hispanic vote is starting to flow the Republican way, isn't it?"

"*Sí.*"

"*Sí* is right, and *sí* is what I say. *Sí* and *muy bien!*"

5

"Next up, G. Man, is JP. He's a Democrat from Santa Monica."

"In the bond of all things red, white, and blue . . . Go ahead, JP. Make my day!"

"Hello, Mr. Hopewell. I'm . . . I'm a first-time caller."

"Welcome aboard."

"I just want you to know . . . It took a lot of courage for me to call."

"Charlie, do we have a badge of courage to send this guy?"

"I'm on it."

"First off, even though I'm a liberal, I agree with you on the three strikes-and-you're-out rule, and on capital punishment as a deterrent and—"

"Well, good. There's common sense on each and every phone line this morning!"

"On the other hand . . . Well, I've been holding this in for a while now and . . . and . . . it's why I finally got up the courage to call and . . . Well, I just can't believe that a sexual predator like Arnold Schw . . . Schwaaahaaaaa—"

"Are you crying? Are you really crying about The Terminator winning that recall election?! Get over it, already! And JP from Santa Monica, you ought to know by now . . . there's no crying on my show. Go hug your Mama, ya little fussamussa! You're gone!"

CLICK!

"I mean, you really think your fellow Californians want a tax on their cars? Get your head out of the sand. Your man Gray just didn't have a clue, and apparently neither do you! Sheesh . . . I hate to hang up on a guy, but some folks just deserve to be cut short. *Click*, just like that. Gone! See ya!"

"And now a word from our sponsor, G. Try not to hang up on them."

All I can say to Arnold: *"Hasta la vista*, baby."
You're not going to be around on Election Day . . .
This campaign is just beginning.

—Art Torres,
California Democratic Party Chairman

The history of American politics is littered with bodies of people who took so pure a position that they had no clout at all.
—Ben C. Bradlee

An ass may bray a good while before he shakes the stars down.
—George Eliot

The ass will carry his load, but not a double load . . .
—Miguel de Cervantes

Chapter Two

Donkey Defined

The Democrats are the party of government
activism, the party that says government can
make you richer, smarter, taller, and get the
chickweed out of your lawn.
—P. J. O'Rourke

9

Rheumy eyes look out over a field that hasn't been turned in years.
Husks like crumpled Dump the Hump flyers crunch underfoot,
and with each step, joints protest; the creaking is two parts sinew,
one part pelt. The animal's skin is as wrinkled as a blue dress in an
evidence bag. A snort escapes the flared nostrils. It is the sound of
too much pride meeting too little success.

This is no elephant. Not a sheep, nor a wolf. This is a donkey,
the original donkey born of Democratic dreams and liberal aspirations.
He's been here since the beginning, growing big and strong on the
finest Bermuda grasses before succumbing to the mental and physical

breakdown that is old age. Now, he surveys the land through confused eyes and does not like what he sees: the Democrats in decline.

The first recorded association of donkey and Democrat was in 1828, when cartoonists parodied President Andrew Jackson for his populist, backcountry ways. He epitomized the Democrats of the time; thus, the jackass was a perfect symbol. Many cartoons showed Jackson trying to lead his stubborn ass (that is, the party) wherever he wanted it to go, even years after leaving office.

One particular cartoonist is famous for cementing the place of the elephant and the donkey—the most recognizable symbols in America, outside of Uncle Sam, Mickey Mouse ears, and the Golden Arches—in politics. Thomas Nast brought the jackass back to life in a *Harper's Weekly* cartoon in 1870. The animal was drawn to represent the antiwar Democrats with whom Nast disagreed. Years later, when *The Herald*, a New York newspaper, was editorializing against President Ulysses S. Grant, he lampooned the paper's editors with a donkey in disguise. The caption read: "An ass having put on a lion's skin roamed about in the forest and amused himself by frightening all the foolish animals he met within his wanderings."

"One of the animals frightened by the donkey's roar of Caesarism," writes congressional historian Ilona Nickels, "was an elephant—a symbol for Republican voters, who were abandoning President Grant, and in Nast's view, about to fall into the Democrats' trap." The elephant had also been used before, but here they were, together for the first time. Other cartoonists picked up on the idea of the elephant and the donkey and, just like that, America's leading political parties had their symbols.

Dictionaries are like watches; the worst is better than none, and the best cannot be expected to go quite true.
—Samuel Johnson

Adrift amidst a lack of party leadership and hungry for something to believe in, the donkey stumbles around the husks and stones, desperate for guidance. He quickly finds a raison d'être, latching onto a light just beyond the edge of this fallow field. His beacon of hope. The donkey, despite his decrepit mind, is able to recall the Gateway Arch in St. Louis, the gateway to the West. Without his old friend Thomas Jefferson, there never would have been a Louisiana Purchase. The West would have been a vacation destination requiring a passport. Those were the good ol' days, he thinks, back when men were men and donkeys were glad.

Donkeys and burros are domesticated asses: in fables the ass is represented as obstinate and stupid.
—*Webster's New World Dictionary*

Back in the day, Friedrich Nietzsche posed this question: "Can an ass be tragic?—To perish under a burden that one can neither bear nor cast off?" Since the ordinary burro has no say in what he is, his situation is indeed tragic. The domesticated, Democratic donkey, on the other hand . . .

Democrats make mountains out of molehills, playing up personal ordeals for their overburdened constituency. They ply their trade in the midst of true tragedy, pretending to have tragic stories of their own to tell, all in the interest of attaining "street cred."[3] They don't do any of this particularly well, yet they continue to somehow get away with it. In the case of the cookie jar that's suddenly half empty, the child feigns ignorance for the mother who is willing to believe because she wants so badly to believe. The Democrats are

11

---

[3] Cred as in "credibility" or "credentials." (Get with it, faithful reader. Turn off *The O'Reilly Factor* and watch some MTV!)

that child, and they have enjoyed Mommy turning a blind eye for far too long. Those cookies, too.

All the old donkey can do is shrug his shoulders and move on. Not cookies, but pure Bermuda grasses for him. Rare is the time he would settle for anything less; he has standards, after all!

His beacon of hope—that light in the distance—has cleaved now, like the division that has run through his party since its inception. The idea of self-interest versus philanthropy has recently replaced the Mason-Dixon Line as that fissure. The wolf and the sheep are threatening to replace the jackass as the party symbol. Is it the end for the donkey? And who is this supposedly stubborn, dimwitted creature, anyway? Would the real jackass please stand up?

I first began looking up curses when I was in the third grade. "Jackass," once discovered, quickly became the put-down of choice on the playground.

More recently, my definition quest led me to borrow a vintage 1970s Encontre Animal Card from a friend. Published by a Japanese company, these collectibles were advertised in the back of comic books, along with x-ray glasses and sea monkeys. Pictured on the front of each card is an animal in action—poetry in motion—much like the old, mail-order *Sports Illustrated* posters. Instead of Dr.

> The secret of the demagogue is to appear as dumb as his audience so that these people can believe themselves as smart as he is.
> —Karl Kraus

J jamming or James Lofton leaping, you might find a red-eyed opossum swinging in a tree, fur the color of Dick Gephardt's wig, or an ostrich burying its head, tail feathers silhouetted against the sky like a bust of Bill Clinton—an anus instead of that bulbous nose staring you in the face.

Reading up on the donkey, I, the aging animalphile, learned about various *asinus* nomenclature. This is the information I missed as a third-grader, back when I was focusing on adjectives rather than nouns, and ordering the x-ray glasses rather than the Animal Cards.

In bold type, right across the top of the card, are the words: "Not as dumb as it's thought to be—quite the reverse!" I'd like to trust this information, but I'm skeptical. Further down, the reminder that a "jack" is a male donkey. And anyone worth their Reference Section salt knows that an ass is not a person who repeatedly makes the same mistakes, but any of the horselike mammals that has long ears and a short mane. With my crew cut, that's kind of how I looked as a kid! And actually, now that I think about it, an ass *is* someone who repeatedly makes the same mistakes. Like William Jennings Bryan running his mouth and running for office, or Hillary Clinton wearing those Crayola-colored pantsuits; like Al Gore trying to be cool.

The card teaches me that donkeys are classified in the phylum *Chordata*, subphylum *Vertebrata*, class *Mammalia*, order *Perissodactyla*, and the family *Equidae*. If Encontre ever decides to put out Political Cards, the world will learn that Democrats are classified in

> Bill is the most sex-crazed man I've ever known. He never seemed to get enough—which was usually fine by me.
> —Gennifer Flowers, making her standards known and her mama proud

the phylum *Discordata*, subphylum *Lackofvertebrata*, class *Nongenitalia*, order *Philanthropactyla*, and the family *Equilibrist*. I'd definitely buy a pack or two of Political Cards, especially if they included a piece of that flat, pink bubble gum!

The history of the Democratic Party is overpopulated by jackasses, but we can't forget the ladies. The aforementioned Hillary, Janet Reno, Madeleine Albright, Geraldine Ferraro, Edith Wilson, Eleanor Roosevelt . . . all could have been named Jenny. That's what you call a female donkey: *jenny* with a "j" and not a "g," because with a g, it becomes *Genny* as in Gennifer Flowers, and the Democrats have other names for *her*, harkening back to those dictionary-diving days of my youth.

Speaking of males and females, a jenny can gestate its baby for up to 385 days. This may seem like a long time, but I'm not surprised. It's perfectly apt, seeing as how the Democrats think of government as one big womb—in the maternal womb for a long time, and then living for a long time in the virtual womb. Currently, the longest-running jackass is the eighty-six-year-old senator from

> Since when is "opportunistic" a bad word in America?
> —Gennifer Flowers, in a *New York Times* interview upon the New York City opening of her show, *Boobs: The Musical*

the state of West Virginia, Robert Byrd. The old guy couldn't keep up with a donkey now, let alone in his youth.[4] From the card, I learn that average land speed for a wild burro is thirty miles per hour. Who knew? Then again, Ted Kennedy has been clocked doing close to the same at many a reception. Ah, the grace and beauty of a man lunging for last call, reliving those glory days at Ha'va'd and getting the most he can out of someone else's tab.

This is the donkey defined.

You have been very highly recommended to us by a number of coaches in your area, and also by our talent scouts as a possible Pro Prospect.
—Green Bay Packer head coach Lisle Blackbourn

I want to go into another contact sport, politics.
—Harvard tight end Ted Kennedy, passing up an offer in 1955 from the Green Bay Packers

---

[4] Speaking of running, Byrd could retire at any time, joining the five other Southern Democrats who stepped down in 2004. Add in Ralph Hall's switch to the Republicans and suddenly the demographics of the Democrats don't look so hot.

Some, it seems to me, elect their rulers for their crookedness. But I think that a straight stick makes the best cane, and an upright man the best ruler.
—Henry David Thoreau

It's not the voting that's democracy, it's the counting.
—Tom Stoppard

By fleeing the state twice, employing numerous stalling tactics and groundless legal action, the Democrats have cost taxpayers untold sums of money.
—Tom DeLay (R-TX), on the Democrat protest over redistricting in Texas

Chapter Three

America's Longest-Running Joke:
The Electoral College

What ass first let loose the doctrine that
the suffrage is a high boon and voting
a noble privilege?
—H. L. Mencken,
as quoted in the *Baltimore Evening Sun*

17

The American political tradition is rife with anomalies that contradict
notions of "each vote counts" and popular elections. One of these is
gerrymandering; the most recent example being Texas Democrats
and Republicans battling over redistricting. When Representative
Ralph Hall switched to the GOP, the Democrats saw the writing on
the wall. And when the Republicans, well within the letter of the law,
made a move toward redistricting, those Democrats, one less in number now, fled the state for New Mexico, so as to rob the House of its

quorum. Before packing their bags, they should have considered this fact: The system of electoral votes and of congressional districts was willed to them by their own party. Only from the mind of a jackass . . .

The root of these anomalies is the Electoral College, and the Electoral College exists because Democratic founding fathers had no faith in the common man. The same party that claims to be in touch with the masses of working classes felt that the nation's nobodies were too uneducated to handle a direct election. They shuddered at the thought of those they hobnob with in American Legion halls and at McDonald's actually choosing the next leader of the free world. In their hands, the popular vote didn't seem so popular.

To be specific, we have the Committee of Eleven to blame for all of this. An offshoot of the Constitutional Convention, these newly unleashed Democrats were charged with devising an agreeable system of election. Hungry for dinner and thirsty for beer, one of the not-so-egalitarian Eleven suggested that they go out. The other ten seconded the motion, and off they went in search of libations.

Optimism filled the air. Stronger still was the sense of being insiders to history. Of course, they had no clue that their legacy would include gerrymandering or, far worse, that so many presidential elections would be a virtual fraud, as the victor was handed the keys to the Oval Office without receiving a majority—or sometimes even a plurality—of popular votes. The Electoral College is the equivalent of the gateway physician—a middle man who

18

makes the process more laborious than it need be. But, riding the tide of a warm May breeze, the Committee of Eleven could practically smell their significance.[5] Nobody knows where the Committee went—nobody even knows who was *on* the Committee—but it's safe to assume that these decisions were reached while under the influence. Otherwise, what excuse is there?

> It is enough that the people know there was an election. The people who cast the votes decide nothing. The people who count the votes decide everything.
> —Joseph Stalin

They arrived at a local public house and got right down to business, ordering a round of beers and calling for a stack of cocktail napkins. Immediately, the ideas began to fly and the quill was dipped.

"Gentlemen, gentlemen!" One stately gentleman cried out. "We need to act like gentlemen!"

All the gentlemen in attendance agreed, and they resumed acting like gentlemen. The first act in this rebirth of all things gentlemanly was to order another round. It should have been clear that nothing good could come of this.

When impoverished people connect with a candidate, make the effort to vote, celebrate that candidate's victory, and then find themselves as deprived as they were before Election Day, of course they're going to eventually lose interest. The fact that poor minorities have voted less and less since the 1960s should be no surprise. This is the Democrats' constituency—or at least it was. As Bill Vaughan said, "A citizen of America will cross the ocean to fight for democracy, but won't cross the street to vote in a national election."

---

[5] When significance has an odor, it is usually the stink of self-importance!

After years of promises made by sheep and broken by wolves, it should be obvious why.

Nobody in the ghetto elects the president, and sure as mayonnaise doesn't belong in recipes, nobody in the Electoral College hails from the trailer park.

Quill met with napkin as the first decision was reached. The gentleman charged with taking notes noted, "Second Place Wins!" and the proceedings went downhill from there.

"In order to prevent Electors from voting only for a 'favorite son' of their own State," writes William C. Kimberling of the Federal Election Commission, "each Elector was required to cast two votes for president, at least one of which had to be for someone outside their home state. The idea, presumably, was that the winner would likely be everyone's second-favorite choice." If that doesn't fill you with confidence in the Committee, I don't know what will. Under their system, the presidency was awarded to the silver medalist. Learning about this original design reaffirms my decision to register as an Independent. Second best will not do for me. I prefer third best.

In 1800, Thomas Jefferson and Aaron Burr won an equal number of electoral votes.[6] The tie, settled in Jefferson's favor by Alexander

> If we Americans are to survive it will have to be because we choose and elect and defend to be first of all Americans; to present to the world one homogeneous and unbroken front.
> —William Faulkner

---

[6] Incumbent John Adams won the majority of popular votes but only got the bronze. Part of the Electoral College formula was counting slaves as three-fifths of a person, a benefit for slave states, as they were awarded more electors.

> Democracy is
> being allowed to vote
> for the candidate
> you dislike least.
> —Robert Byrne

Hamilton and the House of Representatives—in accordance with the rules of the Electoral College and leading to Hamilton's eventual death—was an anomaly never to be seen again. At least, not in the exact same manner. The Twelfth Amendment took care of that.

The idea of the tiebreaker came to the Committee of Eleven after dinner and yet another round. Upon a second cocktail napkin, the gentleman wrote, "House of Reps!"

A majority of the Eleven cheered, "Yea," and the table was set for thirteen years hence, when Jefferson would win the presidency, Burr would have to settle for second fiddle, Adams would have to go home, and Hamilton would end up colder than an American pilsner.

21

In 1824, Andrew Jackson, John Quincy Adams, Henry Clay, and William Crawford each represented a different faction of the all-mighty Democratic Party. The electoral vote revealed no absolute majority, thus none of the four could be named president. The House of Representatives selected John Quincy Adams, even though Andrew Jackson had received more electoral votes than any other candidate. It was the second—but certainly not the last—time in American history that a candidate with the most votes did not win.

Twelve years later, the Whigs showcased three candidates for the presidency. Each—William Henry Harrison, Daniel Webster, and Hugh White—was popular in different parts of the country. The Whigs just assumed that one of their guys would win, but under the Electoral College this was not to be. In short, the jackass struck again, robbing the American people of having a direct say in who would lead them. The Whigs didn't factor in the length of Andrew Jackson's coat-tails, and Martin Van Buren, the vice president under Old Hickory, played the role of incumbent, winning an underwhelming plurality of the popular votes.

The proprietor of that Philadelphia public house certainly recognized the importance of the meeting and, therefore, made sure to pour the beers pronto. Thinking of women all across the country, the waitress tried to deliver hints with each subsequent round. For example, she used her most suggestive voice at one point, stating,

"How *macho* to create something as *powerful* as the Electoral College. The only thing better would be knowing that *my* vote counts. Imagine *me*, a woman, voting for the *president* . . ."

They couldn't imagine it. Instead, the asinus ensemble returned to the brainstorming and beer. They had a country to screw up!

Before the words, "Go West, young man—go West," were ever uttered, one of the Eleven said, "Go left, young man. Go left." Little did he know his directions would not

A mob is a society of bodies voluntarily bereaving themselves of reason . . .
—Ralph Waldo Emerson

The mob has many heads but no brains.
—English proverb

The "In Case You're Ever on *Jeopardy*" Interlude

A "Faithless Elector" is an elector pledged to vote for his party's candidate for president but who ends up voting for a different candidate. This happened as recently as 1988 when an Elector, a Democrat from West Virginia, cast his votes for Lloyd Bentsen (for president) and Michael Dukakis (for vice president) instead of the other way around. Regardless of whether this was an honest (albeit stupid) mistake, no one should know better than the Democrats about being faithless!

While on the topic of Alex Trebek, unbeknown to most Americans, the process of converting popular votes into electoral votes is similar to the way the College of Cardinals selects a pope. If you really want to rid the country of the Electoral College, just make this fact public knowledge!

23

> To say that a man's defamed reputation dies
> with him is to ignore the realities of life and
> the bleak legacy he leaves behind.
> —Justice H. Lee Sarokin, U.S. District Court

only lead one of his fellow Committee members to the kitchen—the gentleman was looking for the back door and the outhouse—they were a foreshadowing of the party's future ideology. Go left . . .

"Go West," would be Horace Greeley's legacy, a motto to sum up the Democrat's "Manifest Destiny" platform. In the election of 1872, Greeley succumbed to despair—after winning a bare handful of states and losing control of his newspaper editorial platform in the bargain—before the Democratic electors could cast their votes for him, and they ended up having to divide their votes among the remaining candidates from the party. Not that it mattered. In the end, the Republican incumbent, Ulysses S. Grant, received the majority of votes and was reelected.

Reconstruction still haunted the nation in 1876, and a depression was on. The Republicans went with Ohio governor Rutherford B. Hayes, he of the buckeye fame, while the Democrats hung their hopes on New York governor Samuel J. Tilden. The third-party candidates, as they are wont to do, drew just enough votes to make the election a real electoral mess.

On election night 1876, Tilden was prematurely announced as the winner. There was no Tim Russert and no whiteboard, but there was Florida, Florida, Florida (as well as South Carolina and Louisiana). The electoral votes of those states had yet to be decided, and unlike 2000, they never would be. Infighting, vote swapping, and more of that brain-numbing beer

> Seriousness is
> stupidity sent
> to college.
> —P. J. O'Rourke

24

are rumored to have been involved, as the nation waited on a decision. Congress assembled a Committee of Fifteen and charged them with doing something, *anything*, with these three states. The Committee handed Hayes the presidency even though Tilden had won a majority of the popular vote, because a deal had been struck to end Reconstruction. Unfortunately, the legacy of the Committee of Eleven and its Electoral College lives on.

It is fitting to use the word "College," since these hijinks call to mind the blunders of underachieving frat boys. The 1888 election made crystal clear that beer and logic do not mix, and that the individual vote does not decide in America. States' rights were so protected under the auspices of the Electoral College that Benjamin Harrison was handed the presidency without receiving the majority of popular votes. Sense a recurring theme here?

Done with their libations and legislations, the Committee of Eleven, eager to sleep it off, paid their tab. The proprietor was happy. He was among the few who would have a vote, even if it was just a popular vote, and counting the currency, he was able to revive his dreams of someday owning a convertible buggy.

> Nobody will ever deprive the American
> people of the right to vote except the American
> people themselves—and the only way they
> could do this is by not voting.
> —Franklin D. Roosevelt

Our position is, no matter what the circumstances, France will vote "no."
—Jacques Chirac, French prime minister

I now inform you that you are too far from reality.
—Mohammed Saeed al-Sahhaf (aka Baghdad Bob), former Iraqi Minister of Information

Chapter Four

Commonsense Radio Network:
Tuesday

I would think that if you understood what
communism was, you would hope, you would
pray on your knees, that we would someday
become communists.
—Jane Fonda, as quoted in the
Detroit Free Press in 1970

27

"Good morning, everyboooooody. Respecting the rights of all American
citizens and convinced that the cream always rises to the top, this is
G. David Hopewell, and you're listening to Radio America! As we
do every day from 6:00 to 10:00 A.M., I'm coming to you live from
the studios of the Commonsense Radio Network, where the reception's clear and so's the logic. Charlie, what do you have for me this
morning?"

> The first Republican I knew was my father. He joined our party because the Democrats in Jim Crow Alabama of 1952 would not register him to vote. The Republicans did. I joined for different reasons. I found a party that sees me as an individual, not as part of a group. I found a party that puts family first. I found a party that has love of liberty at its core. And I found a party that believes that peace begins with strength.
> —Condoleezza Rice,
> addressing the RNC in 2000

"Good morning, G. Man. We've got Larry from Missoula on line four."

"Here's to hoping Larry can start our day on the right foot. In the name of all things red, white, and blue, Mr. Missoula . . . whip it!"

"Into shape! Shape it up! Get straight!"

"Go forward. Move ahead! It's not too late! To whip it! Whip it good! Okay, Larry. You're on. What's up?"

"G. Man, I love the show. No questions, just a comment today. Listen, I'm really tired of people still debating our presence in Iraq. We signed up for a war and guess what? Our opponent gave us one. For a while, at least! Spider Hole Hussein is finished and democracy is coming. So all you Democrats can just save that anti-Vietnam–type rhetoric for the next time Hanoi Jane comes to town! The people of Iraq are free now. Someday, when American movie-goers are being treated to the Kurd version of *Schindler's List*, I'm going to kick any dove I see right out of the theater. All of you who backed down when times got tough, don't start talking about the children Saddam gassed, don't start lamenting the genocide, don't open your friggin' mouth! It's not about oil. It's about people. It's about finishing what we started. And it's about Bush and Rice and everything nice in 2004! Take care, fellas!"

CLICK.

"An obvious Condee fan there, but the man was on point. Larry knows that might is right, that the sword is indeed mightier than the pen. I often worry about how things are going to end up in the Middle East, but you know what? The world is slowly but surely democratizing. And it's all thanks to the good ol' U.S. of A."

"There you have it, G. Man."

"Yes, indeed. That was a good start to the day, Charlie. Who's next on the Commonsense Radio Network?"

"We've got Sunflower in Iowa City. She's waiting on line two."

"You are my sunshine, my only sunshiiiiine. All right, Sunflower, in the name of all things red, white, and blue . . . Make me happy when skies are gray!"

We want it to be very clear that the war on terrorism is not a war against Islam. Islam is a religion that respects innocent human life. So we cannot believe that Islam would countenance the kind of destruction that we saw on September 11th.
—Condoleezza Rice,
in an interview with *Al Jazeera* in 2001

"Skies are gray and only getting grayer, America. And I'm not even talking about Gray Davis, America. Global warming is melting our ice caps, America. Scientists are lying so that Bush doesn't cut off their federal grants, America. Drill—"

"Sunny, dear, if you say 'America' one more time I'm going to cut you off. You're making it sound like a dirty word and I don't appreciate it."

"Every day is Earth Day. Peace!"

CLICK!

"She's gone. She's gone, Charlie? Unbelievable! Isn't it just like a liberal to embrace the drive-by phone call? Well, I'll tell you what, sweet thing, if you want to continue driving around in that Land Rover of yours, the one with not a zebra but a little donkey on the wheel cover, if you want to be able to gas up to follow Phish from state to state, if you want to stay warm during those long Iowa winters, you'd better be prepared to find other sources of oil. And don't talk to me about natural gas and cars that plug in at night. None of that makes any sense. If you understood economics or science, you'd know that, *Sunny!*

"We all know what Clinton was pulling in those last few days in office. While Hillary and Chelsea were loading conch shells and couches, property of the White House, into the moving van, his hand was cramping up from signing all that national park legislation. Nothing but a thinly veiled attempt to cement his place in history, giving thousands of acres away like that. Bush is just reclaiming what belongs to the American people. He wants to boost business and create jobs. And he wants to do it in as safe a way as possible. Scientists just need to be smart about where they drill and where they allow roads to be cut. And I'm sure they will. You ever hear of the trial and error that is the scientific method, Sunflower? I doubt it, because I'm sure that you and all of your patchouli-smelling friends couldn't care less about the money your parents spent on college. If you did care, you would've studied to become an ecologically correct scientist or a common-sense economist. Instead, you scheduled as many afternoon classes as possible, read up on Far Eastern mythology, and just barely managed to get passing marks in that! Good luck with the job at Starbucks, and be sure to call again!"

"Calm yourself, G. The heart, remember your heart."

"All right, doc. Prescribe a conservative caller or two for me and I'll feel much better. Please . . . I know these kooky Democrats are entertaining, but I can't take it anymore!"

Sacred cows make the tastiest hamburger.
—Abbie Hoffman,
one of the "Over 1 Billion Served" at McDonald's

Chapter Five

America's Longest-Running Joke:
From Jefferson to Jackson

There are many things in life that are not fair, that wealthy people can afford and poor people can't. But I don't believe that the Federal Government should take action to try to make these opportunities exactly equal, particularly when there is a moral factor involved.
—Jimmy Carter, thirty-ninth president of the United States of America

33

The donkey's first memory is of a freshly turned field in the years following the Constitutional Convention and that Committee of Eleven. His ears perk up now as he remembers: a voice calling to him through time, booming through a megaphone. "Ladies and gentlemen, introducing the Democratic-Republican Party!"[7] As a member of George Washington's cabinet, Alexander Hamilton had his Federalist Party, so fellow cabinetista Thomas Jefferson came up with a party of his own, tit for tat. The name was meant to be a reflection of the nation Jefferson wanted to build, rather than a reaction to the top-down imperialism he hoped to avoid (thus his discomfort with the name Anti-Federalists).

In his mind's eye, the young foal sees Hamilton on one side of the field, with Jefferson standing on the other. Two of the founding fathers, face-to-face—not dueling so much as debating. Hamilton, ever the aristocrat, liked to write, and he believed, right up until his final breath, that the pen was mightier than the sword. Jefferson also had faith in this quaint notion. Fortunately, Aaron Burr had no beef with him. Otherwise, Jefferson's love interest, Sally

---

[7] Sounds kind of like the Boston Yankee-Sox, doesn't it? The Atlanta Pepsi-Cokes? The Oregon Macin-Softs? The Kentucky Hatfield-McCoys?

> Political correctness is the natural continuum from the party line. What we are seeing once again is a self-appointed group of vigilantes imposing their views on others. It is a heritage of communism, but they don't seem to see this.
> —Doris Lessing

Hemmings, would have become America's first unwed widow. Many a child would have grown up fatherless.

The donkey sways, feeling a chilly breeze like the hands of high-schoolers trying to tip him. But the glowing light and the memories help him keep his feet.

The Democratic-Republicans supported states' rights and they believed in celebrating individuality. If Jefferson had beaten Ray Kroc to the punch, a Big Mac might taste like a cheesesteak in Philadelphia and a cow patty in Phoenix. Time proved differently, though, and today a Big Mac tastes exactly the same no matter where you order it: a cow patty cheesesteak, special sauce, lettuce, cheese, pickles, onions on a sesame seed bun!

The donkey smiles, remembering how Jeffersonian democracy was built on the idea that control isn't necessary. The federal government could and should be limited, because—despite his love of V-6 engines and all things *Maxim*—the average joe is wise, capable of governing himself. Yes, *himself*. This was in the days before the Democrats decided to expand all attributes to include, "himself, herself, or itself." Consider this: For most of their history, the Democrats have been as far removed from politically correct as you can get. And it all began with Jefferson. He is actually the perfect representative for America's longest-running political party. From Jefferson to Jackson and beyond, Democratic presidents, congressmen, governors, and party bosses have owned African Americans. And no amount of PC rhetoric can change this fact. The land of the free and the home of the slave . . .

The old donkey, his head bowed in shame, creaks his way toward that guiding light, the gateway to the lands of the Louisiana Purchase, and wonders what will become of him when his number is called. Will his parts be sold off for glue? Or will he simply be cut down like Alexander Hamilton? Will he be ground up into just another Big Mac? That would be ironic as, unlike all those other wild burros, he's always had the highest of standards.[8] He's always preached the healthy life. Holier than thou burger.

Fights have always been started in the press, but until recent years, they were finished face-to-face. While serving as Jefferson's vice president, and a nominee for New York's governorship, Aaron Burr inflicted that fatal wound upon the mouthy Hamilton. The dispute first began during the presidential election of 1800. In a virtual dead heat, Hamilton chose his old nemesis as the lesser of two evils, his dislike for Burr running deeper than his disagreements with Donkey Tom. The consolation prize was the vice presidency.

36

---

[8] He once snorted incredulously as another donkey pretended to know the difference between grass and fois gras.

> To talk without thinking is to shoot without aiming.
> —English proverb

To be VP has always been like getting voted into the court of the homecoming queen—and Burr wanted to be the one wearing the tiara. Needless to say, when Hamilton's words caused trouble for Burr again in 1804, he got really fired up. This time, it wasn't the presidency at stake; the fact that Hamilton was interfering with Burr's political career yet again was all that mattered.[9]

So, Burr went public with *his* feelings. He gave Hamilton the verbal beat-down, and having talked the talk, he decided to walk the walk. He challenged

---

[9] In a Fourth of July toast, Hamilton wished Burr to "be speedily shipped on board a British prison ship, and exported to the congenial regions of Nova Scotia." Them's fightin' words!

[10] Burr's actions earned him neither the governorship of New York nor the presidency. Rather, he was indicted for murder and would later stand trial, on a separate count, for treason.

Dramatic Interlude

Weehawken Heights, New Jersey . . . The donkey remembers it like a scene in *The Sopranos*, although the two men more closely resembled prep schoolers playing paintball.

There, across the Hudson from New York City, Hamilton and Burr watched smokestacks chalk the air with their productivity. Ships moved in and out of the harbor in the deliberate manner of ants. Lady Liberty's spot was ready and waiting, but she was far from being born. She would also experience a long period of gestation. Rather than shake hands, the two combatants paused to appreciate the nation growing before their eyes. Wingmen stood by, anxiously tinkling change in their pockets. An impartial judge checked the pistols and then began his count. There was steel in Burr's eyes, mere pewter in Hamilton's.[10]

CLICK!

> Gossip is charming!
> History is merely gossip.
> But scandal is gossip made
> tedious by morality.
> —Oscar Wilde

Hamilton to that duel and the rest is RIP history.

After Jefferson's two terms, James Madison was elected. Under him, the Democratic Party continued to enjoy its first heyday ("hay day," if you prefer). Madison had written in *Federalist Paper No. 10*, "The most common and durable source of factions has been the various and unequal distribution of property. Those who hold and those who are without property have ever formed distinct interests in society . . . The regulation of these various and interfering interests forms the principal task of modern legislation and involves the spirit of party and faction in the necessary and ordinary operations of government." He understood the task at hand, what was at the heart of the Democrat's challenge: self-interest versus philanthropy. It was all a lot of mumbo jumbo to the donkey, though. All he knew was that he was well stocked in Bermuda grasses. He was years away from visiting the Statue of Liberty and even further away from turning his nose up at McDonald's for the first time.

Unfortunately, the Democrats were also years away from fighting for the equal opportunity to earn property for all. Of President Madison, historian Howard Zinn writes, "Slavery was immensely profitable to some masters. James Madison told a British visitor shortly after the American Revolution that he could make $257 on every Negro in a year, and spend only $12 or $13 on his keep." Puritan practicality to the extreme.

> This is the curse of the
> liberal wimpathy.
> Conservatives talk of right
> and wrong. Liberals talk of
> strengths and weaknesses.
> —Ellen Goodman

> The seasick passenger on an ocean liner detests the good sailor who stalks past him 265 times a day grandly smoking a large, greasy cigar. In precisely the same way, the democrat hates the man who is having a better time in the world. This is the origin of democracy. It is also the origin of Puritanism.
> —H. L. Mencken

In 1812, the brash young donkey, profiting nicely off the labor of others, allowed the British to get the jump on him. Not only did they form allegiances with various Native American tribes, they began to bolster their ranks by shanghaiing American seamen. Less than thirty years after the end of the Revolutionary War, we were battling the British once more. In 1815, they sued for peace and the war hawks of the day, those wily Democrats, celebrated. (Federalists even referred to it as "Mr. Madison's War.") Not till years later would the party play dove, the donkey trading in his pistol for a peace pipe.

In the meantime, the Democrats remained in power, as one James handed the reigns over to another. Like Jefferson and Madison, James Monroe was from Virginia. Also like Jefferson and Madison, Monroe enjoyed eight years in office. Next up was John Quincy Adams, after cutting his teeth as Monroe's Secretary of State; the two men were instrumental in the formation of the Monroe Doctrine. Not only did this self-authorization

> Slavery is malignantly aristocratic.
> —Antoinette Brown Blackwell, as quoted in *History of Woman Suffrage*

> General Jackson's
> mother was a
> COMMON
> PROSTITUTE!!!
> —Charles Hammond,
> taking mudslinging
> to new heights

help the U.S. to protect its Latin American interests, it opened the door on Manifest Destiny. Needless to say, what you see today is not your Grandpappy's Democratic party.[11]

Adams only enjoyed four years in office, but in 1828 the fifth consecutive Democratic candidate was elected. America chose an outdoorsman, a military man, a conservative from a Southern state other than Virginia, a fellow already armed with a nickname: Old Hickory.

Not to be confused with a brand of beef jerky, "Old Hickory" was a compliment paid to Andrew Jackson by his supporters. It grew out of his original, military-inspired nickname, "Old Hero." Jackson was so mucho macho that he did Aaron Burr one better, winning a duel with a man who'd insulted his wife *and* getting crowned homecoming queen.

Old Hickory also defended another man's wife, minus the swordplay. In 1831, Jackson went to bat for his secretary of war, John Eaton. The wives of his other advisors refused to socialize with Mrs. Eaton. According to these old ninnies, she was a woman of questionable morals. In response to all this gossip, Jackson fired the husbands, so as to be rid of the wives, and then hired all of his buddies as replacements. Being friends, they had back door access to the president; it was as if they could just walk right into his kitchen. Thus, the name "Kitchen Cabinet."

On top of that, he was the first president to recommend the elimination of the Electoral College. There's a catch, though. Just when

40

---

[11] By now, the official name of the party had been shortened to Democrat.

> I draw the line in the dust and toss
> the gauntlet before the feet of tyranny, and
> I say segregation now, segregation tomorrow,
> and segregation forever!
> —George Wallace
> in his 1963 inaugural address

you're ready to respect him, to think of him as an all-right guy, to pay tribute to Old Hickory with a Hurricane or two (he was victorious in the Battle of New Orleans), enter the zinger . . . Jackson, in the Democratic tradition, was a slave owner; (one hundred and fifty men, women, and children worked his plantation). To the casual student of American history, it's probably surprising to learn that many a Democrat, from Jefferson to Jackson, owned slaves. Again, it shouldn't be. Just as it shouldn't be surprising to learn that most office-holding Democrats grew up richer than Richie Rich. Bottom line: From this page forward, don't let tales of racist Democrats throw you for a loop. Jackson was no anomaly. Nor was he simply an example of the times. Fast-forward one hundred and twenty-five years to the reign of Alabama governor George Wallace, and you'll learn even more about the wonderful things that the Democrats have stood for.

In the effort to get re-elected, Jackson balanced out his preference for admitting slave states to the Union with the idea of the biggest party the party had ever known. No, not Mardi Gras—this was the quadrennial convention! And

> I feel conscious of
> having done my duty to
> my red children.
> —Andrew Jackson, on his
> Indian removal policy

so it was that in 1832, the Democrats held their first-ever back-patting and ass-kissing carnavál.

The best part was that an average joe could get himself an invitation, same as all the bigwigs. All he had to do was break thumbs for a party boss, move some furniture for a senator, or draw cold beers for the pollsters and then conveniently lose the tab. It's a tradition that lives on today.

Modern-day Democrats try to control the press at their conventions, just as they tried to control who was allowed into that original Donkeypalooza back in 1832. If you saw a black face there, it meant your next course had arrived. And Jackson would've sooner allowed African Americans than women. Not very democratic, now, is it?

The donkey is tired of hanging his head. It hurts his old neck and makes following that glowing arch too darn difficult. Besides, it's easy enough to rationalize the choices his heroes made, way back when. Guys like Jefferson and Jackson were just trying to make a buck, is all. Maybe get laid every once in a while without having to disturb the sheep. In many ways, those were wonderful times to be a young Democrat. But as he stumbles forward now, the new millennium leaving him in search of direction and purpose, the light exposes more truth than he cares to consider. The donkey knows that he was as guilty as the rest of them, high on life and all the Bermuda grasses that a slave could pick.

It's a damn poor mind that can only
think of one way to spell a word.
—Andru Jaxsin

Did I ever get a nomination? No!
You know why? 'Cause I hadn't played any of
them slave roles, and get my ass whipped. That's
how you get the nomination. A black dude who
plays a slave that gets his ass whipped gets the
nomination; a white guy who plays an idiot gets
the Oscar. That's what I need, I need to play a
retarded slave, then I'll get the Oscar!
—Eddie Murphy, in *Bowfinger*

A model talking about a nuclear power
plant is going to capture a different audience
than a nuclear scientist will.
—Christie Brinkley at the
2000 Democratic National Convention

43

Guilt: the gift that keeps on giving.
—Erma Bombeck

Chapter Six

Commonsense Radio Network:
Wednesday

I don't know. There are many theories about it. The most interesting theory that I've heard so far—which is nothing more than a theory, it can't be proved—is that he was warned ahead of time by the Saudis.

—Howard Dean, spreading rumors that George W. Bush knew about 9/11 before 9/11

"Okay, G. Man. It's time for an otherworldly visit from Roswell's number-one son. On line four, it's—"

"Wayne! Well, in the bond of all things red, white, and blue . . . Rock like Spock and don't be a dork like Mork. Take it, Wayne!"

"Hello, Mr. Hopewell. Hello, Charles. I am here to report that there is a major conspiracy afoot. Cheney and the executives at Halliburton are in cahoots and, to make matters worse, they've paid off Michael Eisner, amongst others. This is all a part of a master plan that was devised in conjunction with Disney and ABC and ESPN to send subconscious messages to Americans everywhere."

"What's the message, and who should be worried, Insane-in-the-Membrane Wayne?"

"The plan is to get every AARP member in the country to donate their Social Security to Ben & Jerry's so that they can develop a Fidel Castro ice cream."

"I see . . . Cigar-and-rum-flavored ice cream. Sound good to you, Charlie?"

"Habana Banana might work."

"Gentlemen, do not joke. Both Ben and Jerry are avowed communists . . . according to my sources. And they are both complicit in the rise of obesity in our nation."

"That's funny. I thought they were philanthropicapitalists and that the problem was undisciplined fat people eating themselves into a state of diabetic stasis!!!"

"No, Mr. Hopewell. Tremendous forces are aligning. Consider this chilling denouement . . . Halliburton is not only interested in brokering this deal between senior citizens and Vermont's

Waste from Ben & Jerry's Ice Cream
company is given to local farmers in Vermont to
feed to their hogs. It is said the hogs
don't particularly care for the Mint Oreo.
—From www.foodreference.com

Finest, but their subsidiary, the KBR company, is rumored to be investing heavily in crematories. Not creamation, as in ice creamation, Mr. Hopewell, but crematories, as in disposing of bodies. All of those AARP members, all of those obese Americans . . . Just think about the profits. The financial potential."

"I'm trying, but I keep getting distracted by images of Charles Manson. You're not Charles Manson, are you, Wayne?"

"Mr. Hopewell, I know for a fact that you were born at two thirty-eight A.M. on December thirtieth, 1949. You are about to turn fifty-five. All of this will affect you. And soon."

"Zzzzzzzzzzzzzzz."

"Please do not snore at me. I listen to your show because it is a forum for the exchange of ideas. My ideas are intended to help you and your listeners. Charles, as well."

"Thank you, Wayne."

"I thank you, too, Wayne. I thank you for entertaining us for five minutes on this Wednesday morning. Work on that other theory you have, the one about me being JFK's illegitimate son, and call back sometime."

CLICK!

"What has that guy been smoking, Charlie? I wonder."

"Don't know, G. Man, but on that topic, we have a concerned smoker on line two. It's Jocelyn from New Jersey."

"Jocelyn, you need to be nice to me because according to Wayne, I only have six days to live before Dick Cheney cremates me. On that note, in the bond of all things red, white, and blue . . . Baby, we were born to run!"

"Hey, G. Man. How you doin'?"

"Mighty fine, thanks. What's on your mind?"

"I'm a bridge and tunnel girl. I just love to go out in New York. Start the evening at some cozy Irish pub and then hit the dance hall scene. But this weekend, I got really ticked off. Why is it I can't smoke in bars anymore? I mean, whatever happened to freedom? I work hard all week, and when the weekend comes, I wanna relax!"

"Lawsuits, sweet thing. Class action, states-footin'-the-bill lawsuits."

"It's a joke. Just another infringement of our basic rights. What next? The return of prohibition?"

"Well, here's my idea . . . Normally, I'd be against any form of government interference, but I think that all of this could be solved with a little tax that makes winners out of everybody. A revenue generator and an affirmation of individual choice . . .

"There's already a sin tax on liquor, so why not put one on the alcohol served in pro-smoking bars? Rather than outlaw it completely, give proprietors a choice. Yes, waiters, waitresses, and bartenders will still be exposed to secondhand smoke, but how happy will they all be when the bar has to close and they're out of a job? The government can't worry about everything. Makes financial sense, doesn't it? Much better than a ban . . ."

"I agree, G."

"Now, do yourself a favor, Jocelyn, and give up the cancer sticks. You'll live longer and smell better."

"Save it, ya old prude! Buhbye!"

CLICK.

To cease smoking is the easiest thing I ever did. I ought to know because I've done it a thousand times.
—Mark Twain

It's fine to be a great democrat when
you've a slave to rub your boots on.
—Christina Stead

Chapter Seven

America's Longest-Running Joke:
Depression and Southern-Fried Discrimination

The Democratic Party is like a mule. It has
neither pride of ancestry nor hope of posterity.
—Ignatius Donnelly,
from *Dictionary of Political Quotations*

Although the old saying goes, "The apple doesn't fall far from the tree,"
the donkey and his friend Thomas Jefferson used to consider their
fellow Democrats and say, "Noooo, the *nut* doesn't fall far from the
tree!" No one remembers what a good sense of humor Jefferson had.
He was the best kind, an optimistic humorist. The donkey misses his
old friend.

Looking back over his long life, he recalls the rut his party fell
into after Jefferson's death. The Democrats just couldn't snap out of it,
doing their zombie's walk around Foggy Bottom and ignoring the most
pressing issue of all. The arrival of Honest Abe, along with secession,

served as the alarm clock in their collective ear. The emergence of a political party to rival them was quite the wake-up call, as well. The Democrats had allowed the slave trade to continue for too, too long, trying desperately to promote the marriage of Northern business and Southern agriculture, and letting it lead to the nastiest divorce in American history.

In the years following Jefferson and all those Jameses, the Democrats enjoyed a virtual monopoly over the White House. In 1837, Martin Van Buren graduated to homecoming queen, making the kind of leap Al Gore can only dream about. Not only is MVB memorable for his ancestry of tavern keepers (maybe even the pint-pouring proprietor of Committee-of-Eleven fame), he had a nickname far superior to Old Hickory. Yes, it's true: We once had a president called "The Little Magician." Poor, poor Mrs. Van Buren. Apparently, the only thing big on Marty was his mane. The missus, by the way, was his cousin, Hannah Hoes. So many jokes, so little time. So little . . .

The hair, though; there was nothing little about that. The Little Magician let his locks grow horizontally, inexplicably cultivating an anti–comb-over, loony-bin look. He was the forefather to convicted congressman James Traficant, and the similarities only begin with their frolicking follicles. There's also the fact that, while the latter is serving time for tax evasion, the former should have served time for continuing the Indian removal policy, including the infamous "Trail of Tears." The Little Magician spent only four years in the White House, and, despite his eight-year sentence, Traficant will probably spend, at most, four years in the big house. Such a proud, proud heritage.

Old Hickory's coattails actually proved long enough for two. At the urging of Jackson, James Polk threw his hat in the ring in 1844 and surprised critics—who'd called the party crazy for nominating him—by making it all the way to the finish line. This was quite a change for Polk, who'd lost in bids to be the governor of Tennessee not once, but twice. The donkey fast-forwards to 2000, wondering, yet again, why Al Gore couldn't even carry his home state. Bush won the popular vote in Tennessee and the eleven electoral votes to go along with it. How can Gore show his face there? How could Polk?

Perhaps because Polk not only won the presidency but served ably, acquiring much of the Wild West, as a part of Manifest Destiny.[12] But where he failed was where the American people needed him

Despite bad suits, bad hair, and bad attitude, Traficant was that little pinprick that kept opening more and more eyes, heretically nudging the most dangerous voting class: the awakened Democrat. Do you know Social Security is screwing the little guy? How about Welfare? Do you know how bad our government waste is? Do you know Dad never got a job working for a poor man? And do you know which party has caused these problems in the first place? Those are the questions that left Traficant nearly friendless at the end.
—Tom Adkins, of www.commonconservative.com

---

[12] More surprising behavior from the donkey: Polk waged an *imperialist* war against Mexico for this territory.

> Slavery is founded on the selfishness of man's nature—opposition to it on his love of justice.
> —Abraham Lincoln

most: bringing North and South together on the issue of slavery. Doing so just wasn't in the cards, though. Kind of like being governor of Tennessee.

In Polk's final year, the Democratic Party centralized, as the Democratic National Committee was formed (they promptly helped him lose the election), and four years later the DNC pushed the reluctant Franklin Pierce into the limelight.

Franklin Pierce Adams (the poet) once wrote, "Too much Truth / Is uncouth." And the truth is, Franklin Pierce couldn't convince his nutty wife to play the role of First Lady. The idea of leaving New Hampshire (New Hampshire?) for Washington, D.C., so upset her that she tried to talk him out of running. This was typical behavior. Pierce had resigned from the Senate after she nagged him about not being home enough. But, for some reason, Pierce accepted the presidential nomination. He refused, however, to campaign, and once

54

> Every wolf in sheep's clothing who pretends to preach the gospel but proclaims the righteousness of manselling and slavery; every one who shoots down negroes in the streets, burns up negro school-houses and meeting-houses, and murders women and children by light of their own flaming dwellings, calls himself a Democrat.
> —Oliver P. Morton, Democrat-turned-Republican governor of Indiana (1863)

elected did not make any changes to the cabinet he had inherited. Pierce just wasn't one to rock the boat: one of the most powerful men in the world, and he had to bring his niece along to social functions, while the missus stayed home. What chance did he stand of swaying Congress?

About as much chance as he had of getting reelected. Actually, the heavy-drinking president couldn't even get nominated again (he was the first president to be denied in this way by his own party). The Democrats ran another James, and after four miserable years, the miserable Pierces went home to the Granite State.

Civil War Interlude

Enter Union blue and Rebel gray, Robert E. Lee's loyalty, Rhett and Scarlett, cannonballs, tattered flags, $300 men, hardtack, Mathew Brady, Matthew Broderick and Denzel Washington, scurvy, Pickett's Charge, Sherman's March, Nicole Kidman and Jude Law, the Appomattox Courthouse, Ford's Theatre . . .

From 1857 to 1861, James Buchanan was the nation's premier vacillator. Back in the day, his type was referred to not as a "fence sitter" but as a "trimmer," and the issue he trimmed on most was slavery. Bucky believed strongly that compromise was the only way the nation could survive and that American citizens *had* to obey the law, even when they found the law to be unjust. If the ACLU were in existence back then, I doubt he would've been a card-carrying member.

Where's my mule? / Where's my forty acres? / Where's my dream? / Mr. Emancipator.
—Warren Haynes on General Sherman's promise of reparations for slaves (overruled by the Democrats)

> The Democrats, for
> their part, played the
> race card relentlessly in
> their own way, charging
> that the radicals'
> Reconstruction policies
> were designed to
> elevate former slaves
> above whites.
> —Jules Witcover

Bucky also thought that questions of morality could not be settled by political action. (There goes his NARAL membership, too.) The country needed a leader who could think outside of the box.

While campaigning, he said, "The great object of my administration will be to arrest the agitation of the slavery question at the North and to destroy sectional parties." Mission: Impossible!

Two days after Buchanan's inaugural address, Supreme Court Chief Justice Taney handed down his Dred Scott decision. Harkening back to the old *Federalist* debates between Jefferson and Hamilton, the Court decided that the Missouri Compromise was unconstitutional and that the government could continue its policy of treating people like property. Buchanan put the icing on the cake when he supported the admission of Kansas as a slave state. War was as imminent as Bucky's impotence was evident. During his presidency, the Democratic Party self-destructed, heading down the byways of American history in small, near-powerless factions. They would walk that road for a well-deserved quarter century.

After the war, the healing process was long and slow, and it took the Democrats quite some time before they were able to shake the moniker of "rebel." It didn't help that they were the party of the Ku Klux Klan or that, up in New York City, William M. Tweed was using the mayor's office, in the grand tradition of so many of his fellow "holier than thou" Democrats, to earn millions via kickbacks. Stealing Tater Tots and padding the personal coffers . . . The

> The lesson should be constantly enforced that though the people support the Government, Government should not support the people.
> —Grover Cleveland, aka The Great Obstructionist

Democrats were desperate for an issue to sink their teeth into, now that the Industrial Revolution was at full steam, but they struggled to find an identity. Their constituency was farmers and poor factory workers (including recent immigrants), but how to unite such diverse groups? No answer emerged, and the Democrats, much like the Democrats of today, floundered.[13]

The drought seemed to come to an end, but the rain didn't last long. Grover Cleveland, who served as president from 1885 to 1889, and then again from 1893 to 1897, lived up to the low expectations portrayed by Thomas Nast's donkey cartoons. He was a bit of a trimmer himself, benefiting from Democrat support as well as a number of rebellious Republicans, called "mugwumps." He lost to Benjamin Harrison in 1889, only to return as a new and improved Independent four years later.

Two minor details before we move on . . . First, in 1886, Cleveland topped both Pierce and Buchanan by marrying his former

> All the world loves a good loser.
> —Kin Hubbard
>
> Show me a good loser and I will show you a loser.
> —Paul Newman, paraphrasing Knute Rockne

---

[13] During this time, the donkey went twenty-four years without feeding from the Rose Garden.

ward, Frances Folsom. (Somewhere, Woody Allen reads this page and smiles.[14]) Wait, it gets better. Cleveland had also fathered a child out of wedlock, prompting Republicans to chant, "Ma, Ma, where's my Pa? / Gone to the White House, ha, ha, ha!" (Woody loves musicals almost as much as he loves his daughter.) Second, Grover, whose birth name was Stephen, had another name, a nickname only a proctologist could love: The Great Obstructionist. With his insistence on the gold standard, not to mention violent strike-breaking techniques, Sir Obstructalot completely mismanaged the country through its worst economic depression to date. Soup kitchens were even dubbed "Cleveland's Cafes." Needless to say, sixteen years passed before America forgot the bitter legacy and gave the Democrats another chance.

Baseball scouts will actually talk of the talent a twenty-game loser possesses, the line of reasoning being that a pitcher must be good for the manager to continually start him. These scouts are miss-

---

[14] Woody Allen: "I want to tell you a terrific story about oral contraception. I asked this girl to sleep with me and she said, 'no.'"

ing something, though. The manager trots this guy out every fifth day because he doesn't *have* anyone better! The same can be said of William Jennings Bryan and his lengthy tenure as the poster child for the Democrats.

The party's lone hero during the years between Cleveland and Woodrow Wilson, Bryan was talented enough to be trotted out for three different presidential elections. He was on the losing end every time. Even one of his friends, a senator by the name of Henry Teller (R-CO), admitted, "If I were a working man and had nothing but my job, I am afraid when I came to vote I would think of Mollie and the babies." The majority agreed, and, remarkably, so did the Electoral College.

Bryan never was able to develop an off-speed pitch, and this led to him losing in a different kind of ball game. When Bryan took to the breach as the anti-Evolution prosecutor in the Scopes Monkey Trial, Clarence Darrow embarrassed him on the witness stand, using Bryan's own testimony to prove that the Bible cannot be interpreted literally. A few days later, Bryan died of tongue-twisted mortification.[15] The donkey hangs his head with the memory, not only out of mourning for his fiery friend (if only he'd watched what he ate; if only he'd developed a change-up), but because those years were so, so bleak for the party. He shudders, remembering how things got so bad at one

He kept us out of war.
—1916 campaign
slogan for
Woodrow Wilson

59

---

[15] That's right. The Democrats once constituted the same religious right that they criticize so harshly today.

> What great cause has ever been fought and won under the banner "I stand for consensus?"
> —Margaret Thatcher

point that he'd almost resorted to eating scrub brush. Almost.

The new century brought with it the usual blind optimism, and—after years of abject mediocrity—the Democrats were confident that they'd found a keeper in the gentleman intellect Woodrow Wilson. After doing his best to keep the U.S. out of the Great World War, he contradicted his campaign promises, and the U.S. stormed Europe like an ace closer in the ninth inning of a one-run ball game, helping the Allies to defeat the Triple Alliance and to end the war to end all wars. Looking back, it should have been clear that Wilson was more of a water boy than a twenty-game winner. As with Cleveland, his successful run at the presidency had been made possible only because of an act of Republican rebellion. Teddy Roosevelt splintered the GOP vote when he joined up with the Progressive Party and, in a spoiler effort similar to Ross Perot's in 1996 and Ralph Nader's in 2000, his party's constituency diluted itself. Theodore Rex handed Wilson the keys to the White House.[16]

Wilson had worked hard to elevate himself from professor to university president to New Jersey's governor to president of the United States of America, but his lack of clout was fully exposed as the League of Nations, his postwar baby, died a quick domestic death and a long,

> This treaty might get by at Princeton but not at Harvard.
> —Senator Henry Cabot Lodge (R-MA), Harvard graduate *(Veritas!)*

---

[16] Yet another presidential election where the winner did not receive a majority of the popular vote.

> There are blessed intervals when I
> forget by one means or another that I am
> President of the United States.
> —Woodrow Wilson, overjoyed twenty-eighth
> president of the United States of America

painful death abroad. Wilson was like Pierce with his wife or The Little Magician with that loony-bin hair. Everything was out of his control.[17] The years he'd spent overseeing the staff and students at Princeton did little to prepare him and, as we are seeing today, the Senate was wise to doubt the legitimacy of an international peace-keeping body.

And for those still not convinced that Wilson was more cream puff than closer, how about this: He remains the only U.S. president to ever allow a Mexican invasion. The joke has long been that the Salvation Army could defend our borders against Mexico or Canada, but when Pancho Villa killed a couple of Americans in Chihuahua in 1916, and then capped it off by raiding Columbus, New Mexico (where he murdered more Americans), next to nothing was done about it. General John Pershing was sent into Mexico to extract revenge, but to no avail. The donkey's reaction was not action but words: He vowed to never again let anyone call him "burro." He cared not to be reminded of this embarrassment (and that his bray was worse than his bite). Jackass was even better in his eyes; there would be no more talk of burro!

> I pledge you, I pledge
> myself, to a new deal for
> the American people.
> —Franklin D. Roosevelt,
> thirty-second president of
> the United States
> of America

---

[17] On the bright side, he didn't date his niece or marry his foster daughter.

Since the New Deal, Democrats have emphasized the role of the federal government in promoting social, economic, and political opportunities for all citizens. They generally support a tax system that places a greater burden on the rich and large corporations, and they prefer spending on social programs to spending on defense.

—E. D. Hirsch

Wilson faded to obscurity as a stroke lamed him during his lame-duck year. Rumors swirled about his wife assuming the role of president, keeping Vice President Thomas Marshall from seeing the president and prompting Senator Albert Fall (R-NM) to say, "We have a petticoat government! Mrs. Wilson is president!" In 1924, Wilson went to his reward, and the Democrats would have to wait until 1933 to see the Lincoln Bedroom again—unless they took the tour.

To this day, Franklin Delano Roosevelt remains one of America's most memorable presidents. This doesn't mean that he is without fault. FDR *is* the father of modern-day Democratic rhetoric; he embraced big government of Hamiltonian proportions. Paradoxically, it is the way that he treated minorities and civil liberties that is inspiring me to "go teacher" on him. African Americans, as well as the Nisei and Issei, had a legitimate beef with the pride of Hyde Park, and therefore, so do I.[18]

---

[18] The "Nisei" were U.S.-born American citizens whose parents had immigrated from Japan. Under FDR's orders they, along with the "Issei" (first-generation Japanese immigrants not excluded by racist law, yet eligible for U.S. citizenship), were placed in internment camps.

Before describing the low points of FDR's record-setting four terms, the beating he took in 1920, running as the vice presidential candidate with James Cox of Ohio, deserves a mention. The GOP tag team of Harding and Coolidge dropped the proverbial hammer on them, to the tune of 60.4 percent of the popular vote and 404 electoral votes. Joe Tumulty, a Democratic party boss, declared, "It wasn't a landslide, it was an earthquake." Wilson's coattails didn't lead to the World Series; they led right back to the sandlot. But not to worry; FDR would rise like the phoenix from the ashes of Black Tuesday.

Speaking of ashes, it was FDR who initiated "Fireside Chats." But that's not the reason for this transitional statement. No, what I'm getting at here is that long black cigarette holder of his. Heiresses don't use cigarette holders. Metrosexuals fresh off a manicure don't use cigarette holders. Even lepers don't use cigarette holders! I can only think of two people who use them, and they are both cartoon characters! First, there's The Penguin, one of Batman's fiercest foes. The second is the villainess in *101 Dalmatians*, Cruella DeVille.[19] What man aspires to be like a bird that can't fly? Or to look like a skunk-headed dog hater? A man who likes to chat by the fire, I suppose.

In the 1930s, the donkey tried to do the cigarette holder thing, but set his stash of Bermuda grass on fire. (Plus, there was the opposable thumb thing.) He could afford the

We shall tax and tax, and spend and spend, and elect and elect.
—Harry Hopkins, WPA administrator

Bums are the well-to-do of this day. They didn't have as far to fall.
—Jackson Pollock, in a letter to his father (1933)

63

---

[19] The Cadillac Eldorado is another convertible I wouldn't mind driving . . .

> A government that robs Peter to pay Paul can
> always depend on the support of Paul.
> —George Bernard Shaw

Bermuda grass and the cigarette holder because, like most wealthy Democrats, he'd kept his money well protected in the years leading up to, and during, the Great Depression. He has never been, as relentlessly advertised, a typical American. He was no Tom Joad.

Financially speaking, World War II came along at just the right time. And so FDR was invited to stick around, once more, in 1944. The nut doesn't fall far from the tree, though, and, like Wilson, his health failed. In 1945, he died exhausted, leaving millions in mourning—all except for African Americans who'd served in the segregated military, only to return home to find friends and family still being strung up like strange fruit. Truth be told, Wilson and FDR both blew off anti-lynching legislation. Doesn't make for a great epitaph . . . Also not to be seen among Roosevelt's mourners were the Japanese Americans who'd been forced to live, for three years, in his internment camps. Even when they were allowed to return to their homes—if they were fortunate enough to still have their homes—an understandable feeling of distrust permeated.

"The news of being able to go back to California has been accepted with mingled feeling," wrote Fusa Tsumagari. "Those with property are wanting to go back, but wondering how the sentiment will be."[20]

This is one of FDR's legacies, and, although the Democrats prefer to ignore it, the idea that they are the champions of the under-

---

[20] In 1988, a congressional study determined that America's internment policy stemmed from "race prejudice, war hysteria, and a failure of political leadership." Subsequently, Ronald Reagan signed the Civil Liberties Act, which granted $20,000 to each surviving internee.

dog does not hold up well. The criticisms relating back to big budget and big government do, though, especially when evaluating the lasting impact of FDR's presidency.

British Prime Minister Harold Wilson said that, "One man's wage increase is another man's price increase." Too many Democrats have yet to learn this lesson. The wage increases have not been absorbed by businesses; they have been absorbed in price increases and in greater government spending. The increase in government spending has meant, of course, increases in taxes. And in dependence.

The donkey didn't mind. He had his money—more than enough to cover the Bermuda grass and that stupid cigarette holder—but Hamilton must have been cheering in his grave as all that New Deal legislation was passed. By the midway point of the twentieth century, government agencies had become employers on par with today's Wal-Mart.

You are a king by your own fireside,
as much as any monarch on his throne.
—Miguel de Cervantes

I'm not the smartest fellow in the world,
but I can sure pick smart colleagues.
—Franklin D. Roosevelt, chatting by the fire

Clinton made a stop in Chicago yesterday, continuing his cross-country farewell tour as the president. The tour was an emotional one, as it may be the last time for thousands of young Americans to see their father.
—Craig Kilborn, on
The Late, Late Show with Craig Kilborn

You know, if I were a single man, I might ask that mummy out. That's a good-looking mummy!
—Bill Clinton, discussing Juanita, an Inca mummy discovered in 1996

I lived a dream life (almost too exclusively, perhaps) when I was a lad, and even now my thought goes back for refreshment to those days when all the world seemed to be a place of heroic adventure in which one's heart must keep its own counsel.
—Woodrow Wilson, dreaming of those glory days

They dream in courtship, but in wedlock wake.
—Alexander Pope

Chapter Eight

Smoke and Mirrors and Steamboat Willie—Dream or Nightmare?

> A deck of cards is built like the purest of hierarchies, with every card a master to those below it, a lackey to those above it.
> —Ely Culbertson, bridge player and author

67

Going teacher sure takes a lot out of you. I'm almost afraid to rest, though, as this dream I've been having might come again. Some nights, it seems so real . . .

It's poker night, and Madeleine Albright is hosting. Crudités, Pizza Rolls, and pigs in a blanket. Billie Holiday on the hi-fi. A postcard from Prague and the cover of Bill O'Reilly's latest book, complete with the crudely drawn rings of a bull's-eye, are stuck to the fridge. The fun gets underway with a volley fired Bill Clinton's way: Joyce Elders asks him to take an oath before she deals the first hand. Hijinks.

As with any friendly game of poker, the clueless (and soon-to-be penniless) sprinkle themselves among the savvy. To the loser goes the dishwashing duties. To the victor goes the spoils.

Before fifteen minutes has passed, the eventual victor—the only man in attendance—lays his cards facedown and bluffs to lose. William Jefferson Clinton is in his element.

"I don't know . . ." He stretches to full length, trying for a game of footsy with Janet Reno. His fingers still rest atop the fan of cards. "Nope. Can't do it. I fold."

Three hands later, he continues setting the table for himself, going so far as to reveal what he's holding. It's just one of his strategies: honesty with a purpose. "I tell ya . . . I've got a pair in the hole, but without three of a kind, I don't stand a chance against you girls." Dramatic pause, then the decision to fold once more. "Wild card or no wild card, better safe than sorry." After Donna Shalala takes a $2.25 pot with three threes, he tosses a compliment her way—there's some business he'd like to discuss later. "Gutsy by you, not so gutsy by me. No guts, no glory, right?"

"Belly but no guts?" Madeleine offers. Janet opens her mouth to speak, but he gives a reassuring wink. By now, she's used to defending him.

Yes, Slick Willie is in his element, stogie jutting out well beyond his Leno-like chin, arms crossed in good-natured resigna-

Gennifer Flowers, when asked if she had the
same type of relationship with
Bill Clinton as Monica Lewinsky did,
replied, "It was close, but no cigar!"
—www.freakyhumor.com

A hard dog to keep on the porch.
—Hillary Rodham Clinton, referring to her husband

tion, and playable cards sacrificed during the nickel-and-dime rounds. After another bout of affectionate needling, he relights his cigar and addresses his pals.

"The cards will come. Eventually . . . And yes, I still stand by what I said. Like this here cigar, I did *not* inhale!" To call Bill Clinton an extrovert would be like calling Michelangelo artistic. To say he enjoys the spotlight would be like saying Homer Simpson is fond of the occasional donut.

Donna asks, "Opinions, ladies?"

"Guilty as charged!"

There's a tittering uproar. Madeleine, also folded, needs the diversion. As with any gathering of colleagues, she's eager for her guests, now that they've arrived, to go. Although the card game has been on for less than an hour, she's already down $13.60.

"I'm innocent!" he cries.

Madeleine shakes her head, a coy smile playing across her supple lips. "You'll never be innocent, William. And you'll never, ever change."

Janet hopes with all her heart that he doesn't. Not ever. Even as she wags a finger, her oedipal love swells. She's up $6.75 at this

> The other thing we have to do is to take seriously the role in this problem of older men who prey on underage women . . . There are consequences to decisions, and one way or the other, people always wind up being held accountable.
> —Bill Clinton

point and feeling the warm glow of her second Pilsner Urquell. By profession, Janet can sniff a liar out in seconds flat, but with him it just doesn't matter. When you can tell tall tales and still leave them smiling, you're a charmer. And Janet, she thinks he's a real charmer.

"I wouldn't inhale on your cigar, either, Bill."

"Oh, Janet," Madeline says. "You've too much experience. William here isn't looking for aged wine. He prefers bottles of Bud with born-on dating."

"Dating is right!" He jokes, rubbing Janet's back.

"Dating?" Joyce asks. All these years and she's still smarting from the way he handled her suggestion that masturbation be a part of the health curriculum. "Wasn't it you, Mr. President, who said that, 'Politics gives guys so much power that they behave badly around women. I hope I never get into that.'?"

"Meeee? Couldn't be!"

Through the haze of smoke and laughter, images of the doctor's daughter abound.

> It was a real sort of Southern deal. I had Astroturf in the back. You don't want to know why, but I did.
> —Bill Clinton, describing an El Camino he once owned

No one names their daughter Monica anymore. Certainly not any of the Democrats.

Janet and Madeleine had talked about it once, and they agreed: It was the risk that attracted him, like a high-schooler swilling Wild Turkey before class. And their Bill was one wild turkey.

Clinton just loves the attention and, in the glow of Madeleine's recessed lighting, he can appreciate not only the banter but the way Donna's close-cropped hair shimmies and shines. He'd asked Madeleine to invite her because of her position; her location. The president of a university? In southern Florida? She'd definitely be able to hook him up with some good times. Janet, Donna, Carol Browner—all of his Miami connections are here. Nothing is coincidental with Steamboat Willie.

The former leader of the free world is really warming up now, winning a hand here and there and making more of those down-home, self-effacing pronouncements. "Get a loada me. Worst player at the table and I'm actually even now. So, back to that little matter before . . . I never inhaled and believe me, you. I never smoked *that* cigar!"

> I've said I've never
> broken the drug laws of
> my country, and that is
> the absolute truth.
> —Bill Clinton

71

> Donna Shalala is quite short and rounded, which belies the adage that successful women MUST be tall, willowy, and blonde.
> —Irene Stuber, on www.singlemomz.com

Joyce and Carol have both been working on getting him to quit smoking—smoking cigars and telling his awful jokes. It isn't easy getting a wild turkey to go cold turkey, though.

"Speaking of cigars, let me try that Cuban of yours."

"But of course!" He'll always say yes to Madeleine. Whatever it is she's asking, the access he has to her makeup artist makes it well worth it. Besides, Madeleine has a special place in his heart, being so much like his mama and all.

Forever sophomoric, he watches her take a puff and wants to shout, "Oral fixation!!!" She smiles like she can read his mind, which, for all intents and purposes, she can.

Alexis Herman pipes up. "Can we play cards, please?"

She's also one of his favorites: a powerful female minority willing to push the fund-raising envelope. What more could a guy ask for?

"Let's go, people!" Her eagerness leads the savvy to surmise that she has to have a winning hand. But Donna sees the $1 and raises her another $2.

"It's your pot," Alexis concedes.

"Mmmmm, your pot," Bill echoes, looking Donna's way. Hint, hint. Then he goes to his second favorite comedic foil: Al Gore. "You know that Al's son isn't the only one in the family to smoke, don't you? I've heard that, back at Harvard, my former wing-

> If the dress doesn't fit, we must acquit. If it's on the dress, he must confess.
> —Congressman James Traficant, Jr. (D-OH)

man used to smoke *his* share, riding his motorcycle in that black leather jacket and acting like an extra in *Easy Rider*. Boy, did he go from dude to prude!"

"Al *is* a bit on the uptight side, isn't he?"

Bill feels like Carol is also one of his more successful pet projects. A graduate of Miami-Dade Community College, she could probably set him up locally should things not work out with Donna. He's so consumed with his own plotting and planning that he never realizes how much these women have also played him over the years. There's a reason Carol was the longest-running EPA administrator in history. She knows—they *all* know—how to stroke his ego.

"You don't know the half of it, Carol. I mean, Al and I . . . We were like oil and water. To him, Arkansas's just one big breeding ground for toothless bastards, and here he was, riding around on Air Force One with one. His boss, no less! All along he thought he should be the president, and then what's he do? He blows it. I mean, come on, man! You let Bush's kid beat you?! By the way, well played, Donna. Well played."

"Thank you, Mr. President."

> Marijuana is . . . self-punishing. It makes you acutely sensitive, and in this world, what worse punishment could there be?
> —P. J. O'Rourke

> Treat people right and the rest will take care of itself.
> —Benny Binion, owner of Las Vegas's Binion's Horseshoe Casino, before IRS agents seized all of the casino's property

> If he had asked me to continue the game
> of hearts back in his room at the Jasper
> Holiday Inn, I would have been happy to
> go there and see what happened.
> —Nina Burleigh, White House correspondent,
> discussing a game of hearts with Bill Clinton on
> Air Force One

Bingo!

"Ah, the things we could've accomplished with just four more years. Me and my ladies against the world. No cabinet of men could've done it any better!"

"William, calm yourself. We all know you're no feminist," Madeleine stares into his soul, playing her hand perfectly. The only thing a man like Clinton wants more than a risk is his mama. "You play with us because you think you can beat us, and you think you can beat us because we're women."

"I play with you because I think you're *all* so beautiful, Madeleine. And smart, of course. I mean, you're my posse." Showboat Willie is a player in every definition of the word. *Beautiful?* To bluff on a 5, 6, 7 would pale by comparison. He's the kind of condescending bastard that they've been chewing up and spitting out since grade school. Yet, for personal gain and an occasional good time, they allow him to play his game (and even to tell his jokes). "Besides, this is fun. My Mama used to tell me, 'Never eat at a place called Mom's. Never play cards with a man called Doc. And never, ever sleep with a woman whose troubles are worse than your own!'"[21]

---

[21] Compliments not of Virginia Kelley but of Nelson Algren.

"You'd be hard pressed to find a woman like that." Alexis has never forgotten that this is the same man who once said, "African Americans watch the same news at night that ordinary Americans do." He did a lot for her career, but in terms of being a great civil rights leader, she has some serious doubts. "Hey, Mr. President . . . What do you get when you cross an ambitious lawyer and a crooked politician?"

"I don't know, Alexis." And he really doesn't. "What do you get when you cross an ambitious lawyer and a crooked politician?"

"Chelsea!"

Touché.

The game goes on and, like that Committee of Eleven, Janet has a few too many. Bill knows he'd better get to her soon for that legal advice. Meanwhile, Donna leaves the table to watch the big game: Miami versus Florida State. He decides that he'll broach the topic with her if and only if Miami wins. The rest of the ladies stay around the table, and, black hole that Clinton is, more and more of their money gets sucked his way. He hits an inside straight and sweeps up the chips, piles and piles of red, white, and blue rising before him, as the stogie dwindles to a stub. He tells them about his office in Harlem, slipping in an old, tasteless Father's Day joke—Joyce and

I'm fed up! Fed up playing Greek chorus to your rehearsed nightmare!
—Samuel Fuller

It's a hard choice, but I think, we think, it's worth it.
—Madeleine Albright, discussing the report that over a half-million children had died as a result of sanctions against Iraq

> For Clinton, draft ducking, toking on a marijuana cigarette, and a family life that he acknowledges has not been perfect create the same effect: He is unable to establish moral authority with opponents who might otherwise be open to his centrist style and policies.
>
> —Jim Hoagland

Alexis share a look—and, after taking a particularly large pot, decides he'd better cover himself by feigning inebriation.[22]

"This German dude, Ludwig Fulda . . . Well, he said that you're still the king, even in yer undies. And I believe that. I really do! Look at y'all . . . Who needs money an' power when ya got such buttiful friends? I'm the kinga the world!!!"

A master of goodwill, Clinton keeps tabs on his compliments the same way he counts cards. But deep down inside, what he loves most about these ladies is that they know how he is, and yet they still hang around. That's power. It's not just about bringing home the nickels and dimes. No; it's about building relationships and profiting in quarters and half-dollars sometime down the road. That's the Steamboat Willie way.

On the last hand, a barrage of betting that involves some minor league cursing and some major league bluffing, Arkansas's number-one son wins a pot worth a whole $11. It takes them seven minutes to play out the hand of Texas Hold'em, but it only takes him thirty seconds to tally his booty.

---

[22] In 1997, balancing the budget was so important to Clinton that he went against the wishes of those he now calls "neighbor," axing $5 billion in funding for school repairs and allowing the Senate to reject a plan that would provide health insurance to more than ten million children.

"I sure do love it! Hey Donna, how'd it go?"

"My boys won . . . Bill, when you're done playing, I need to talk to you about something."

"Sure. How 'bout *now?*"

It goes better than he ever could have hoped. She wants him to be a face for the university. Her goal is to turn the U of M into the nation's largest research institution. To hook him, she dangles this simple tidbit: "One of our goals is the development of a legally acceptable form of tetrahydrocannabinol. THC, Bill."

"Medicinal marijuana?"

"Exactly."

Donna has played her hand perfectly. The biggest fund-raiser the school has ever had is now in her back pocket.

Like nuts falling from the tree, the ladies drop away from the table as they realize he's through for the night. Madeleine sees her opportunity and flicks the lights. They all promise to do this again, real soon.

"Call me about that divorce advice, Bill!"

Madeleine can't help but smile at Janet's inappropriate outburst.

He who permits himself to tell a lie once, finds it much easier to do a second and third time, till at length it becomes habitual; he tells lies without attending to it, and truths without the world's believing him. This falsehood of the tongue leads to that of the heart, and in time depraves all its good dispositions.
—Thomas Jefferson

The front door clicks securely, and finally, she has him all to herself. Hosting and a makeup artist are a small price to pay. "It's time to up the ante, William."

Democrats—the way they conduct themselves . . . You'd have to inhale to enjoy that kind of life. What a nightmare.

Any president that lies to the American
people should have to resign.
—Bill Clinton,
during the Nixon investigations

Can you believe there's only two days left
in the Clinton administration?
Boy, time flies when you're having sex!
—Jay Leno, on *The Tonight Show*

I got very well acquainted with Joe Stalin, and I like old Joe! He is a decent fellow.
—Harry S. Truman, thirty-third president of the United States and a good judge of character

The atom bomb was no "great decision." It was merely another powerful weapon in the arsenal of righteousness.
—Harry S. Truman, thirty-third president of the United States and a good judge of the value of life

Chapter Nine

America's Longest-Running Joke:
Hawks in Dove's Clothing

I'm not big enough for the job. I'm not big enough. **81**
—Harry S. Truman, thirty-third president of the
United States and a good judge of self

Up until the day he died, FDR worked hard to cast the modern-day Democratic die. The donkey was still a son of the conservative South, though, when Roosevelt's vice president, Harry S. Truman, grudgingly took oath.

Truman is best remembered for giving the *Enola Gay* its marching orders. The U.S. had only to let the emperor retain his honorary title and Japan would have surrendered, but Truman decided to go with the big bombs, anyway. Wilson had the pleasure of knocking in the game-winning run in World War I; Truman pitched a perfect ninth to close out World War II.

> Arguments are to be
> avoided; they are
> always vulgar and
> often convincing.
> —Oscar Wilde

Truman had gained political prominence when, as the vice president, he uncovered millions of wasted dollars in war contracts. Refreshingly unaware of what it means to be a wingman, not only was he critical of FDR's war expenditures, he called the New Deal legislation mere "cosmetics," and felt that the Great Depression had petered out of its own accord. Truman had more faith in business cycles than in the alphabet agencies.

In a nutshell, Truman was against spending money domestically, but in favor of spending it abroad. Approving the Marshall Plan in 1952, he went against his conservative nature—contradicting himself in true Democrat style—when he approved a $13 billion package for Europe, enemies and allies alike. A wonderful gesture of philanthropic proportions, but what do we have to show for it? Mercedes-Benz makes some fine, fine convertibles (the SL class defies description) and Oktoberfest is Mardi Gras with lederhosen, but come on—the Cold War lasted for more than four decades, Harry. And FDR spent too much?

The donkey's head spins as the confusion of those postwar years returns to him. Closer now to that glowing arch of truth, justice, and the *asinus* way, the donkey gives up on trying to label Truman. Conservative? Liberal? It's just too hard—has *always been* too hard—with all of them.

In the mid-twentieth century, there was still a fissure running

> His primary allegiance was to the party,
> not to an ideology.
> —Robert J. Donovan, referring to Harry S.
> Truman in *Conflict and Crisis*

through the heart of America. Appalling to the modern-day donkey is the acknowledgment that at one point, Southern Democrats put their stock into segregationist Strom Thurmond. There are plenty of Democrats the donkey cares not to see on his family tree, nut or no nut.

At its 1948 DNC convention, the party fell apart. Hubert Humphrey sent Southern

> It is idle to think that a Europe left to its own efforts would remain open to American business in the same way that we have known it in the past.
> —General George Marshall, forming his plan

---

[23] According to Douglas Miller and Marion Nowack, authors of *The Fifties*, Truman's, "commitment to victory over communism, to completely safeguarding the United States from external and internal threats, was in large measure responsible for creating that very hysteria."

Good Ol' Fashioned Political Debate Interlude

Point: Truman's "Berlin Airlift" was pretty ballsy.

Counterpoint: He was where the buck stopped while McCarthy was on his witch hunt.[23]

Point: Red Scare, Red Shmare!

Counterpoint: It was Truman who fired Douglas MacArthur.

Point: Hey, MacArthur used one of those cigarette holders, too! Besides, Truman fought in World War I, so he knew what he was doing.

Counterpoint: The Truman Doctrine started as a $400 million request . . . for Greece and Turkey alone!

Point: He ordered the desegregation of the military.

Counterpoint: It was his fault Chiang Kai-shek got booted out of power in China.

Point: Hey, without Korea we never would've had "M*A*S*H."

Counterpoint: He helped create NATO.

Point: Okay, okay. Uncle.

> A shadow has fallen upon the scenes so lately lighted by the Allied victory . . . From Stettin in the Baltic to Trieste in the Adriatic, an iron curtain has descended across the Continent.
> —Winston Churchill

delegates scurrying to the new, Thurmond-led Dixiecrat Party when he pronounced, "There are those who say to you: 'We are rushing this issue of civil rights.' I say we are a hundred and seventy-two years late. There are those who say: 'This issue of civil rights is an infringement on states' rights.' The time has arrived for the Democratic Party to get out of the shadow of states' rights and walk forthrightly into the bright sunshine of human rights." Well it was about time, boys, considering the party had done the same darn thing nearly one hundred years before.

But life, liberty, and the pursuit of happiness was still a long way away, and even when the Democrats finally agreed to make minorities a focus of their platform, it was just another thinly veiled attempt to add to their constituency. The shift was too little, too late.

The donkey hangs his head even lower with memories of bombs and fire hoses and dogs baring fangs. He and his fellow Democrats had given Martin Luther King Jr. little reason to consider them allies. Speeches like Humphrey's provided a hint of belated healing, but wholesale change was still years away. Years and years; like watching grass grow. Like watching an old, crippled donkey make his way.

> To err is Truman.
> —Martha Taft,
> wife of Senator
> Robert Taft (R-OH)

Harry S. Truman shocked the nation by defeating Dewey in 1948, and then disappointed when his administration lost the "Cold War"—not the arms race with the Soviets, but the temptation of owning a deep freezer. These expensive gifts, offered by businessmen seeking government contracts, were welcomed with open arms by Bess Truman and a military aide.[24] Truman's secretary even got a mink coat. Good thing, too. Life was about to get awfully cold for the Democrats.

In 1952, the DNC put all of its eggs in Adlai Stevenson's basket. They had high hopes for the non-Strom, urban-appealing, oh-so-quotable statesman. Stevenson had been instrumental in the formation of the United Nations, and went on to be elected the governor of Illinois. These highlights were not enough for a majority, though. "I Like Ike" trumped "You Never Had It So Good," and all Adlai could do was whine about the commercialization of the campaigns.

First, the ketchup bottle quote. And then, "This isn't Ivory Soap versus Palmolive." Madge agreed, but gave her vote to Eisenhower, anyway.

> You know, you really can't beat a household commodity—the ketchup bottle on the kitchen table.
> —Adlai Stevenson, on running against General Dwight D. Eisenhower

> After four years at the United Nations, I sometimes yearn for the peace and tranquility of a political convention.
> —Adlai Stevenson

---

[24] The businessmen became known as the "Five Percenters," as their gifts guaranteed them 5 percent of all government contracts.

> Communism is not love. Communism is a hammer which we use to crush the enemy.
> —Mao Zedong

In the era of air raid drills and bomb shelters, nobody was going to vote for a peacenik with a degree in internationalism. Not with the idea of missiles aimed not by us but *at us* running through the nation's head. A man named Adlai just wasn't going to cut it.

After eight years of Ike, John F. Kennedy put the football down, combed his Robert Redford hair, and squeaked his way into the Oval Office. He was the pride of Massachusetts. So young. So dreamy. The aging donkey smiles as he recalls JFK's hair. Van Buren and Traficant could have learned a thing or two from him. That man had *style!*

While taking a walk on one of Cape Cod's glorious beaches, hold a conch shell to your ear and hear a thousand Democrats whispering about the nepotism of the Republican Party. Then dash the blasphemous conch to the rocks as I offer up the head . . . of Bobby Kennedy! Based upon his experience helping Joe McCarthy tar and feather suspected communists, JFK was willing to bring his kid brother into the fold as his campaign manager, and then attorney general. This, despite the fact that Bobby was only thirty-six years old and shared in the DNA that would someday cause John John to fail the bar exam twice before managing to eke out a passing score on the third try.

Primary rival Hubert Humphrey said of them, "I feel like an independent merchant competing against a chain store . . . Kennedy is the spoiled candidate, and he and that young, emotional, juvenile Bobby are spending with wild abandon." Humphrey was eventually rewarded for his service with a domed stadium in Minneapolis, while Hyannis Port's number-one sons went on to be assassinated. With all of these dead Kennedys, how can I possibly make fun? It's hard, so instead I'll issue a caution to the remaining family members. Never

> We took the Kennedys to heart of our own accord. And it is my opinion that we did it not because we respected them or thought what they proposed was good, but because they were pretty. We, the electorate, were smitten by this handsome, vivacious family . . . . We wanted to hug their golden tousled heads to our dumpy breasts.
> —P. J. O'Rourke

ride in a convertible (especially not mine!), never cut through the kitchen, and never pilot a plane at night. Forgetting about politics might not be a bad idea, either. Or, if you insist on honoring the family ghosts by staying in the game, why not get a really, really big Austrian guy to represent you all in office? Nobody will mess with him (especially if he's a Republican).

Amid the sea-salt breezes, even the conch shells refuse to whisper about hypocrisy of a different, more lewd nature. But the truth is, JFK made the most of his years in the public eye, scratching the seven-year itch of a made man's wife and convincing a beautiful East German spy to drop her Iron Curtain for him. Now that's what I call a good Catholic! And to this day, my Cuban father-in-law still has some choice words for JFK in regards to the Bay of Pigs.[25] This

> Now I can go back to being ruthless again.
> —Senator Robert F. Kennedy (D-NY), after winning election

[25] A hawk in dove's clothing, as soon as JFK took office, he increased defense spending by almost 20 percent, adding $9 billion to the budget. Unfortunately, it took him a long time to learn how to use all his new toys.

> While you're saving your face, you're losing your ass.
> —Lyndon B. Johnson, thirty-sixth president of the United States of America

teacher recommends that, from now on, the Democrats do their homework before meddling in foreign affairs. For every Kennedy lost in the line of public service, fifty Cubans were killed because JFK didn't bother to review the invasion plans.[26] Nice work with the Missile Crisis, but when those CIA-trained Cubans were cut down by Castro, the blood was on the hands of Mr. Profiles in Courage. The rise and fall of Camelot was certainly Shakespearean, right down to the award-winning performance that JFK gave as Lady Macbeth.

On that topic, JFK paid tribute to Andrew Jackson when he booted some "red children" (Seneca) off their reservation in upstate New York. The treaty that created the reservation had been signed by none other than George Washington. But a dam needed to be built, so JFK did as he had done in Cuba: He blindly followed the advice of a jackass adviser, and trusting people suffered for it. An ass is someone who repeatedly makes the same mistakes . . .

> Being president is like being a jackass in a hailstorm. There's nothing to do but stand there and take it.
> —Lyndon Johnson, once again using his favorite word in the dictionary

---

[26] Four American pilots, flying unmarked jets, also perished. JFK would later say, "How could I have been so far off base? How could I have been so stupid?"

> On Wednesday, President Bush named the Justice Department headquarters after Robert F. Kennedy. Then he went around the corner and named a strip club after Ted.
> —Jay Leno, on *The Tonight Show*

And another thing—how can you run a country if you can't even ask the right guy to be your running mate? JFK and RFK simply assumed that LBJ would be A-OK with getting the "whatdoyousay?" but would then decline in favor of staying in Congress. (The offer of the vice presidency was simply a kiss-up to get LBJ's endorsement in the South.) But in no way, José, was LBJ A-OK with wanting to stay. He was so happy when RFK made his proposal that he broke down and cried. Then it was time for RFK and JFK to shed some tears of their own, because there was no way to take back the offer. Had the brothers known they'd just "elected" the thirty-sixth president, a Texan even more stubborn than the most stubborn of jackasses, they probably would've called for Ethel and Jackie to come and share in the bawling. Talk about the dam bursting—it was a regular Blubber Fest in the land of conch shells and clam diggers. And all for the electoral votes of Texas.

In terms of that fissure, JFK did his best Honest Abe imitation, trying to balance human rights and passable legislation. As civil rights marches on Washington were being planned, he worked with MLK to keep the proceedings peaceful, but this was difficult, given all of the church bombings and unemployment

> Let's face it, I appeal best to people who have problems.
> —Robert F. Kennedy, campaigning for president in 1968

> I have more influence over members of the U.S. Senate than I do over Billy.
> —Jimmy Carter, frustrated big brother

(in 1963 it was just under 5 percent for whites and nearly three times as much for minorities). So much for *satyagraha*[27] and the legislative process—both men ended up on the losing end of a bullet. Ironically, so did JFK's civil rights rival, fellow Democrat George Wallace.

After that fateful day in Dallas, LBJ made the effort to continue the Democrat tradition of quelling civil unrest while keeping big government alive. He met with some success, domestically, but his foreign policy was more dysfunctional than an AOL chat room. In 1965, two different Americans set themselves on fire in a show of solidarity with the Vietnamese monks. "LBJ, LBJ, how many kids did you kill today?" is not what a president wants to hear when he steps out of the bulletproof limo. Increasing the number of troops *in*, not to mention the number of bombs dropped *on*,

90

> A blue-ribbon panel headed by former presidents Gerald Ford and Jimmy Carter came up with a list of ways to improve the next presidential election. Are these the best guys for the job? Ford and Carter; I mean, between the two of them, they could only win one election.
> —Jay Leno, on *The Tonight Show*

---

[27] Gandhi's policy of peaceful resistance.

> Teddy Roosevelt once said, "Speak softly and carry a big stick." Jimmy Carter wants to speak loudly and carry a fly swatter.
> —Gerald Ford, thirty-eighth president of the United States of America

Vietnam only made matters worse (so bad, in fact, that LBJ didn't even run in 1968).[28] It just goes to show how wrong it is to assume that Democrat = dove. Jackass or wolf is much more appropriate.

Stevenson had ketchup, Humphrey had chain stores, and LBJ had "guns and butter." This was the catchphrase for his presidency, because he was so sure that he could win the war while also dealing with domestic issues. Unfortunately, the butter spoiled and the guns didn't shoot straight. Not under Johnson's watch. But who would take the reins? The donkey's stomach growls as he remembers those tumultuous times. It was just so much easier when the Democrats simply ignored the cries of the common man: Vietnamese, Japanese American, African American, and just plain ol' average joe American.

Bobby Kennedy was born in New York, so he chose that state to make his run first for the Senate and then for the White House.[29] Unfortunately, Sirhan Sirhan got to him in Los Angeles, and the Kennedy family was once again mired in tragedy.

> I've looked on many women with lust. I've committed adultery in my heart many times. God knows I will do this and forgives me.
> —Jimmy Carter, in an interview with *Playboy*

91

---

[28] Seven million tons of bombs were dropped on Vietnam, more than the total for WWII.

[29] Soooo, I guess Hillary wasn't the first to use New York as a launching pad.

> The Democratic Party could no longer hope for
> political success by playing Robin Hood.
> —Jules Witcover

Tragedy of a lesser scale would cast its pall across ABBA–era America as Jimmy Carter won the 1976 election over Gerry Ford. Bad enough was America's decision to give the governor of Georgia a try, but to follow it up by sixteen years later inviting another Southern Democratic governor to lead the country was almost inexcusable.

America should have learned from the buffoonery of Billy Carter.[30] America should have learned after waiting for even or odd days to buy their gas. America should have learned after the Shah was welcomed with open arms and after the debacle of the hostages in Iran; after the Boat Lift Cubans were greeted with all the peanuts they could eat and all the Billy Beer they could drink.

America should have learned after hearing this: "Government cannot solve our problems. It can't set our goals. It cannot define our vision. Government cannot eliminate poverty or provide a bountiful economy or reduce inflation, or save our cities, or cure illiteracy, or provide energy." What, exactly, does government do then, President Swatalot?

Clearly, discussing the Georgia flag with the NAACP did little to prepare Carter for those feisty Iranian college students.[31] Given the insouciance of his "government cannot" quote, it doesn't sound like he was quite prepared for the urgency of the Oval Office.

When the ball dropped on the 1980s, Carter was shown the door faster than Elian Gonzalez. Reagan-Bush gave the GOP

---

[30] "It's the best beer I've ever tasted. And I've tasted a lot!" Billy Carter, promoting Billy Beer.

[31] It didn't help him in dealing with African Americans, either. The rate of unemployment for black youths was an incredible 34.8 percent in 1977.

twelve years in the White House, bookended by two men who made spin doctoring an art: Carter practicing it (turning dove for his campaign even though he'd supported Nixon's bombing in Vietnam), and Clinton perfecting it ("These encounters did not consist of sexual intercourse. They did not constitute sexual relations as I understood that term to be defined."). During Clinton's tenure, doctoring the spin nearly replaced baseball as the national pastime. He wasn't quite as ethical as the future Nobel Peace Prize winner, but he sure did know how to manipulate the press. That being said, the peanut president and the penis president did have quite a bit in common . . .

So, Carter the Incumbent lost in resounding fashion to The Gipper in 1980.[32] And as tradition would have it, the nation needed more than a decade to recover from the latest big-toothed jackass.

When Billy Joel sang about honesty, Walter Mondale made the mistake of listening. Did he really think that saying, "Taxes will go up," would get him elected? In 1984, Mondale lost every state save his own (Minnesota), and choosing Geraldine Ferraro as a running mate didn't help.[33]

Yes, someday soon there will be a woman in the White House (and not just an intern doing deep knee bends, either), but looking back, the only female candidate with less of a chance than Ferraro was Al Sharpton's old running mate, Lenora Fulani.

Ferraro's husband, John Zacarro, might very well have been Jim Traficant in disguise, and even Ferraro was questioned about underpaying her taxes. The icing on the cake came a few years later

---

[32] Reagan-Bush won 489 electoral votes; Carter-Mondale won 49.

[33] Reagan-Bush won 525 electoral votes (including 56 percent of the female vote); Mondale-Ferraro won 13. Just when you thought it could get no worse than 1980!

> Modern life is confusing—no "Ms take" about it.
> —Geraldine Ferraro

when Ferraro's son, known at Middlebury College as "The Chemist," was convicted for dealing cocaine.[34] But the Mondale-Ferraro campaign was doomed before all of these skeletons up and walked out of her closet.

Mondale's finest moment came with some yuks during a debate in Atlanta. After letting Gary Hart speak his piece, Whacky Wally capitalized on a popular Wendy's ad: "You know, when I hear your ideas, I'm reminded of that ad, 'Where's the beef?'" Laughs all around, the donkey included. Little did anyone know that Mondale would soon be gone from the political scene, or that Hart's beef would cause such a big problem four years down the road.

Even more comedic than Mondale was Michael "Unibrow" Dukakis. Before the liberal from Taxachusetts got the nod at the 1988 DNC convention, Hart held a commanding lead. He was actually up by 20 percent when the nation learned of the good ship *Monkey Business*. Hart's heart had swelled amorous as the struggling actress, Donna Rice, plopped down on his lap and made nicey-nice. Next thing you know, Hart's campaign was flushed down the crapper and out to sea.

Unibrow's campaign against George H. W. Bush had some memorable moments, as well. Letting Willie Horton out of jail as a part of the Prison Furlough Program was one—having a hand in rape and murder never makes for good press. Then there was that photo of him sitting in the tank. Only Harvey Fierstein piloting a Stealth would look stranger. Dukakis in that big helmet . . . If he was going for the green Greek Pez dispenser look, well then, Mission: Accomplished! But the presidency turned out to be Mission: Impossible! for Iron Mike. Bush went for the jugular, and the Republicans got themselves another four years in the White House.

---

[34] Unlike John John, after serving four months under house arrest, The Chemist passed the New York State bar exam.

As part of his ongoing financial disclosures,
Jesse Jackson told the *Chicago Sun Times*
this week that he doesn't have a checking
account or a credit card. Probably because
to get those, you need a job.
—Tina Fey, on *Saturday Night Live*

The final two decades of the twentieth century saw some real doozies emerge in the Democratic Party. The donkey has to shake his head in wonderment. For example, Al Sharpton tried playing both sides of the coin as he repeatedly told anyone willing to listen that he was finally running away for good. Or at least until he was shown some appreciation. Some respect. Some love! Despite his penchant for sweat suits, the running never lasted long. Sharpton always returned to the roost, usually just in time to lose his bid for nomination. Then there's Jesse . . .

Jesse Jackson's Rainbow Coalition would turn out to be quite profitable—for Jesse. Not only did it get him access to world leaders, it got him access to the ladies. Talk about forming a coalition! Cut from

Jesse Jackson's in trouble. They're going
after this tax thing. Jesse said he will amend his
taxes to show the money that he paid to his
mistress. See, he has just one mistress. Jesse uses
the standard mistress deduction. As opposed
to Clinton, who had to itemize.
—Jay Leno, on *The Tonight Show*

> I think the black community can separate his personal from his public life, but his effectiveness as a mainstream spokesman has more or less been neutralized.
> —Clarence Page

the same moral-religious cloth as Clinton and JFK, Reverend Jackson didn't have to look any farther than the office to find his affair.

He even joined the ranks of Strom Thurmond, Thomas Jefferson, and Grover Cleveland when it was revealed that he'd had an illegitimate child with an aide.[35] If you like to walk on the sunny side of the street, turning lemons into lemonade, as the Democratic spin doctors are wont to do, you can look at Jackson's news in this way: finally, it could be said that equality had been achieved in America. A black man had—wham, bam, thank you, ma'am—joined the ranks of the political elite! Way to go, Jesse.

Ever the eloquent speaker, he addressed the issue thusly: "This is no time for evasions, denials, or alibis. I fully accept responsibility and I am truly sorry for my actions." I wonder, though . . . Was he sorry about having the affair (and subsequent daughter), or was he sorry that *The National Enquirer* ratted him out?

Either way, Jackson proved that you just can't keep a good man down. The nation learned that he would continue to fight the good fight when he showed up in

> I hear that melting-pot stuff a lot, and all I can say is that we haven't melted.
> —Jesse Jackson, in a 1969 *Playboy* interview

---

[35] The affair took place while Jackson was counseling Bill Clinton. "He was really one of President Clinton's closest spiritual advisers. He went to the White House and prayed with President Clinton," said George Stephanopoulos. You just can't make this stuff up!

Here's the worst part about this whole thing.
During the impeachment trial, Jesse Jackson was
Bill Clinton's spiritual adviser. In fact, that's where
Bill and Monica got that cigar. Jesse was passing
them out: "Here you go! It's a girl! It's a girl!"
—Jay Leno, on *The Tonight Show*

A check or credit card, a Gucci bag strap, anything
of value will do. Give as you live.
—Jesse Jackson, campaigning in Aspen

Jackson was carrying on his affair while he was
counseling President Clinton during the Monica
Lewinsky scandal. In fact, he even brought his
pregnant mistress to the White House, one can
only assume to show off to Clinton how to
properly destroy one's career and reputation.
—Jon Stewart, on *The Daily Show*

Illinois to protest the expulsion of several high school boys who'd
started a riot at a football game. Then it was revealed that he'd used
his influence to help keep open E2, a popular nightclub owned by a
friend's son. This is the same club where, soon thereafter, twenty-
one people were trampled to death when security guards used pep-
per spray to break up a fight. Nothing civil about fighting for those
rights. Even the arthritic, near-Alzheimic donkey has to agree.

Somewhere, Dr. King is shaking his head in shame. And he's had a lot to shake his head about recently. Another embarrassment to Democrats was Washington, D.C.'s mayor, Marion Barry. What did he tell his constituents after being arrested for smoking crack with a prostitute? "Goddam bitch set me up!" Only in America could the capital city be led not once but twice by such a man.

In 1992, there were no soaring saxophone solos to welcome Bill Clinton into office. He received less than 50 percent of the popular vote, and during the campaign one oft-sighted bumper sticker read: "If God had intended us to vote, he would have given us candidates!" (Like Al Gore, Bob Dole suffered from guilt by association.)

William Jefferson Blythe IV was born on August 19, 1946. After his father died, his mother married Roger Clinton, and thus little Billy got a new last name. Following in his namesake's footsteps (Jefferson, not the surname), he would ascend to the presidency after years of intellectual discourse—safely riding out the Vietnam War in England on a Rhodes scholarship that precluded inhaling—and several trysts.

What did we learn from Clinton? We learned that, yes, it *is* possible to be the president and still underachieve. The man is obviously both smart and charming, which is why it makes it very hard to understand his choice in wife, vice president, and various mistresses. Talk

We were trying to figure out how deep the wound was and whether we had to go for radical surgery right away, or if we had time to stabilize the patient and keep moving.
—George Stephanopoulos, when news of the Clinton-Flowers affair broke during the 1992 campaign

It is bad enough that our president is guilty of having an extramarital relationship with one of his young interns. But it is much more damaging that this president looked the American people in the eye and knowingly lied to us.
—Representative Tom Delay (R-TX)

When Bill Clinton blows his taxophone, America will be singing the blues.
—George H. W. Bush

Getting caught is the mother of invention.
—Robert Byrne

about a trimmer . . . In the "I Like Big Butts and I Can(not) Lie" category, Clinton takes the cake. In the underachieving category, as well. For example, who comes up with an idea like, "Don't ask, don't tell?"

> I think it is an unfortunate effort to try to find scapegoats rather than to come to grips with what he has done. And for the sake of the presidency, and for the country, I think it would be a good thing if he recognized and acknowledged his wrongdoing with respect to the judicial process.
> —Kenneth Starr

I suppose it's a tribute to Clinton's cleverness that he got away with all that he did, but what has the man done since leaving the White House? Other than opening an office in the heart of Harlem, his philanthropic side has refused to show itself.[36] Perhaps this is because of the legal bills that still linger from his impeachment hearings. Or maybe it's the $850,000 he agreed to pay to Paula Jones, in an out-of-court settlement.

In 1999, the U.S. House of Representatives voted for two articles of impeachment against Steamboat Willie. Article One, which was "perjury before the grand jury," passed with a vote of 228-206. Article Three, "obstruction of justice," also passed, 221-212.

Republicans might have christened Clinton a sexual liberal, but when it came to appoint-

> I am going to say this again: I did not have sexual relations with that woman—Miss Lewinsky.
> —Bill Clinton, the day before his 1998 State of the Union address

---

[36] Whatever happened to his concern for health care? Peace in the Middle East? AmeriCorps? The Southern boy probably doesn't know it, but by moving into Harlem he's merely sped up the gentrification process, pushing impoverished residents further away from their jobs in Manhattan as the rents rise.

ing justices to the federal courts, he was just to the right of being a trimmer. According to the *Fordham Law Review*, between 1993 and 1996 Clinton's appointees "favored liberal decisions in less than half of their cases." And is it really in line with the donkey's platform to sacrifice social welfare for a balanced budget?[37] According to historian Howard Zinn, at the time of Clinton's 1996 reelection, forty million Americans had no health insurance, minority infants were dying at twice the rate of white babies, and "the life expectancy of a black man in Harlem, according to a United Nations report, was 46 years, less than that in Cambodia or the Sudan." And still, the minority vote was all his. He was selling lies in a buyer's market, but still managing to get top dollar.

> America's greatest strength, and its greatest weakness, is our belief in second chances, our belief that we can always start over, that things can be made better.
> —Anthony Walton

At least Clinton was up front about his choice of "punishment over prevention," dedicating $8 billion to prison construction while expanding the scope of capital punishment. NAFTA was signed, against the wishes of labor unions, and Clinton's welfare-to-work legislation would've knocked FDR right out of his wheelchair. This cost Clinton the support of *The New York Times,* and only the threat of impeachment made his return to their pedestal possible. If Howell Raines could mistake Jayson Blair for a reporter, I suppose the *Times* could also mistake Clinton for an honest liberal.[38]

---

[37] Remember trying to go to the Statue of Liberty or some other national park during the three weeks that he shut everything down? Not a highlight of American history, by any means. Partisan politics, to a T.

[38] Is that an oxymoron?

And the worst part is, the Clintons aren't through. Not by a long shot. Gore may have shunned them in 2000, but Bill is still thrilling fans from Harlem to Martha's Vineyard, and Hillary's popularity is at an all-time high. She finished first in a 2003 *USA Today* / CNN / Gallup popularity poll for women. She received only 16 percent of the vote, but this is, of course, more than enough for an Electoral College win. Jay Leno quipped, "Women admire her because she's strong and successful. Men admire her because she allows her husband to cheat and get away with it!" Condoleezza Rice also made that list, and one can only hope for a Clinton-Condee cat fight in 2008. Better than the Super Bowl is what that would be!

Walking into the rotunda in the Capitol, a group of citizens broke out into spontaneous applause. That tells me, more than anything, that we did the right thing, that the Constitution is alive and well and was strengthened by the impeachment process.
—Congressman Bob Barr (R-GA)

Hillary Clinton is the junior senator from the great state of New York. When they swore her in, she used the Clinton family Bible. You know, the one with only seven commandments.
—David Letterman, on
Late Show with David Letterman

Clinton had become the Democratic Party candidate in 1992 with a formula not for social change but for electoral victory: Move the Party closer to the center. This meant doing just enough for blacks, women, and working people to keep their support, while trying to win over white conservative voters with a program of toughness on crime and a strong military.
—Howard Zinn, in
A People's History of the United States

Book lovers never go to bed alone . . .
—Anonymous

Chapter Ten

Literature for Little Rock

Literature is mostly about having sex
and not much about having children.
Life is the other way around.
—John K. Van De Kamp

When I am dead / I hope it may be said /
"His sins were scarlet / but his books were read."
—Hilaire Belloc

Although there are rumors of Bill Clinton appearing in the next Bond film, and although he's always had Hollywood in his back pocket, it is actually literature that lies nearest and dearest to the former president's heart. Good, clean, wholesome literature.

In anticipation of the grand opening of Little Rock's Clinton Presidential Center and Library, a local office building—called, appropriately enough—the Cox Creative Center, has made an exhibit of Clinton's favorite books. Number one on the list is his wife's auto-bore-ography, *Living History*. Here are some other notable titles:

I Know Why the Commerce Department Sings by Maya Angelou

Masturbations by Marcus Aurelius

The Denial of Buddy the Dog's Death by Ernest Becker

Parting the White Waters: Years and Years of Jim "MacDrunk" MacDougal Stories by Taylor Branch

The Four Brunettes by T. S. Eliot

Inedible Ham by Ralph Ellison

Queen Elizabeth's Soiree: The Story of a Rhodes Scholar and One Wacky Night at the Palace by Adam Hochschild

The Imitation of Rich Little by Thomas A. Kempis

One Hundred Years of Cuban Attitude by Gabriel Garcia Marquez

Immoral Man and Society: A Humorous Look at Getting Caught by Reinhold Niebuhr

Homage to Home Fries by George Orwell

The Evolution of Salutations: An Introduction to Introductions by Carroll Quigley

The Confessions of Mrs. Starr by William Styron

Politics as a Vacation by Max Weber

Nonzero: The Logic of Ordering Two Big Macs and a Diet Coke by Robert Wright

Why Would You Go Home Again? by Thomas Wolfe

The Collected Poems of Bill "The Fox" Foster by William Butler Yeats

In response to the opening of this "lie-brary," a Counter Clinton Library is being built just down the road.[39] On the website, the CCL's founder, an ex-congressman from New York by the name of John LeBoutillier, even lists the near-fifty people Bill Clinton didn't have to pardon in his final, hand-cramping days in office. He didn't have to pardon them because they'd recently died. If not by suicide or gunshot wounds to the head, then in plane crashes. LeBoutillier and his partners, united by the desire to keep Hillary and Bill from returning to the White House, aren't pulling any punches.

But back to the books . . . Seven of the Democratic candidates for the 2004 election have been published in recent years. Their work will not be included in the Clinton Library, for one, because no one has ever read any of these self-promoting tomes and, two, because the proprietor of the Clinton Library gift shop doesn't want to sell schlock. What would garner a greater turnout—a rally for Dennis Kucinich, or a class-action suit regarding the title of his book, *A Prayer for America*—since Kucinich didn't have a prayer of winning the nomination? And would *you* be happy if you bought something titled *Amazing Adventure*, only to learn it had been written not by Hemingway but by Hadassah?[40]

Literature must become Party literature.
Down with unpartisan litterateurs! Down with the
superman of literature! Literature must become a
part of the general cause of the proletariat.
—Vladimir Ilyich Lenin

---

[39] A sister Counter Clinton Library is planned for Washington, D.C., as well.

[40] During the 2003 holidays, Ingram Book Group, the world's largest book wholesaler, reported that only seven copies of *Amazing Adventure* were on order.

Chip Fleischer, publisher of Steerforth Press, writes that, "The candidates' books can be divided into two broad categories. The first is pure campaign fodder focused on issues and autobiography, which covers Dr. Dean's *Winning Back America*, John Kerry's *Call to Service*, Dennis Kucinich's *Prayer for America*, and Al Sharpton's *Al on America*. The other books have a more narrow focus: Wesley Clark's *Winning Modern Wars*, John Edwards's *Four Trials*, an account of his experiences as a medical malpractice and personal injury lawyer, and Joseph Lieberman's *Amazing Adventure*, an account of the 2000 campaign." They may not be featured in the Clinton Library, but you ought to be able to find some copies on the fifty-cent table at the next library spring-cleaning sale. Stranger than fiction is the story of the donkey . . .

Books are fatal: they are the curse of the human race. Nine-tenths of existing books are nonsense, and the clever books are the refutation of that nonsense.

—Benjamin Disraeli

I think it's about time we voted for senators
with breasts. After all, we've been voting
for boobs long enough.
—Claire Sargent, senatorial candidate
from Arizona

Nobody will ever win the Battle of the Sexes.
There's just too much fraternizing with the enemy.
—Henry Kissinger

Chapter Eleven

Commonsense Radio Network:
Thursday

A man would prefer to come home to an unmade
bed and a happy woman than to a neatly made
bed and an angry woman.
—Marlene Dietrich

111

"Good morning, everybooooooody! Respecting the rights of all American citizens and convinced that the cream always rises to the top, this is G. David Hopewell, and you're listening to Radio America! As we do every day from 6:00 to 10:00 A.M., I'm coming to you live from the studios of the Commonsense Radio Network, where the reception's clear and so's the logic. In the bond of all things red, white, and blue . . . Well shake it up, baby, now. Shake! It! Up! Baby!!! What do you have for me, Charlie?"

"G. Man, it must be a full moon. On line four we've got everyone's favorite teen überfeminist . . ."

"Oh boy! Mad Dog, is that you?"

"Yes. Yes, it is!"

"Ah, my one and only cheesehead girl. Nobody cares like the Mad Dog cares, so all of you eligible bachelors in the Madison area, beware!"

"That's right, I care, Hopesmell. And nothing you can say will make me care any less."

"Faaaantastic. Now, why don't you let everyone in on what you care so much about."

"You, with all your fascist ways. You, with all your sexist innuendoes. You, with all your schemes, your loophole-finding accountants, your golfing buddies, your disregard for the environment and the pending extinction of the African Swallow . . . You'll never win, Hopesmell. I'll see you in hell before that happens."

"I already have a table for two reserved, so bring your appetite, my friend. For those of you who don't tune in regularly, Edith 'Mad Dog' Qznicky, like Wayne from Iowa City, calls us at least once a week to spew her venom. We let her go on because she's usually so entertaining. Today, though, she seems to be a bit off her game. Forget to take your pills this morning?"

"Like your colleague, Mr. Limbaugh?"

"See? That's the Mad Dog we know and love! Now, try and be entertaining, young lady. Otherwise, you go the way of the African Swallow."

"I'm calling because this week I apply to college, Mr. Hopewell. And . . . and as a respected adversary, I was wondering if you would write me a recommendation."

"Well now, that's a first, wouldn't you say, Charlie?"

"I think so, G. Man."

"Convince me, Mad Dog. Show me that your logic is precise and your case deserving. Make a Democrat out of me, and I'll consider writing you that letter. You go, girl!"

"Well, first of all, I know that you're a caring man. And the Democratic Party—well, it's the party for caring people."

"Zzzzzzzzzzz."

"All right, all right. You've got a daughter, right?"

"Yep."

"Well, your daughter is like me. A womyn with a 'y.' A womyn in the making."

"Grace is seven! Girl with a 'g.' Grace with a G. G like me!"

"My point is this, Mr. Hopewell: The Democratic Party is the party for those that care about womyn. It's the party that stands up against the Christian right so that we can control our own bodies. It's the party that shows concern for the economic handcuffs our sisters wear the world over. It's the party that is concerned for the Muslim womyn who are being marginalized every time they are told to remove a veil. Suffrage is not—"

"Now wait just a fussamussa minute! You were doing a decent job until the veil. Are you trying to tell me the way we're liberating those ladies is undemocratic? That they want to spend the next three thousand years wearing those veils? Grow up and smell the coffee! It's not like those veils are Vera Wang or whoever it is you kids dig these days! You—"

"Hopewell, I am completely free of materialistic want, so Wang

Jazz is the big brother of the blues. If a guy's playing blues like we play, he's in high school. When he starts playing jazz it's like going on to college, to a school of higher learning.
—B.B. King, strumming Lucille and hoping Mad Dog can get over her sophomoric blues

means nothing to me. Ralph Lauren, Tommy Hilfiger, Calvin Klein, Donatella Versace, neith—"

"Mad Dog, that recommendation is slipping further and further away. Not only is the veil angle two degrees left of ridiculous, how can you tell me—with what Clinton and Jackson did—that the Democrats respect women? If it were up to those jackasses, all women would still be barefoot and pregnant!"

"Mr. Hopesmell, fashion means nothing to me, but equality does. And I know it does to you, too. You could join us in the fight for more than just equal pay. As Ewald Nyquist once said, 'Equality is not when a female Einstein gets promoted to assistant professor . . . Equality is when a female schlemiel moves ahead as fast as a male schlemiel.' So there!"

114

"Now that's entertainment. That's the Mad Dog we know and love! I'm no closer to being a Democrat, but at least you have me smiling."

"Well good, schlemiel. You know I'll still call from college, don't you?"

"One can only hope. Right, Charlie?"
"Indeed."

At best, most college presidents are running
something that is somewhere between a
faltering corporation and a hotel.
—Leo Botstein, president of Bard College

"And I can't wait till high school's done. I know that there are political science professors just dying to mold this mind of mine."

"I bet there are, those child-molesting jackasses . . . Can I say 'jackass' on radio, Charlie?"

"No, but you've been so good lately."

"Oh, and I've been published before. Did you know that, Mr. Hopesmell? In *Bonfire*. That's our school literary magazine. I wrote about cheerleaders and the ozone layer. Mr. Henderson said it was 'an inspired piece.' My mom bought two copies."

"How could I have missed it?"

"So, what do you say? I may have been born angry, but I'm working on being more positive, aren't I? I wouldn't embarrass you. I'd never let you down. Besides, my mom says I'm cute. Do you think I'm cute?"

". . . . . ."

"Your silence speaks volumes and I don't care. I am more than just another pretty face. I am a brain. A fine mind, so kiss my behind! Now, how about that recommendation?"

"Speaking of school, shouldn't you be in class, Ms. Qznicky?"

"My first class hasn't started yet. Did you know I have a ninety-three average? And that I interview well? I can even be pleasant when I want. On top of that, I *am* cute. Brown will have to admit me. If not Brown, then Swarthmore. Or maybe Hampshire. Somewhere where

Women should be obscene
and not heard.
—Groucho Marx

> I'd hate to be a teetotaler. Imagine getting up in the morning and knowing that's as good as you're going to feel all day.
> —Dean Martin

the liberal mind is embraced. You and your beloved Yale can just shove it. I wouldn't want to go to that stinky school, anyway. Not even if it's where John Kerry went and Hillary and Bill met. Hillary's breaking the patriarch mold and I will, too."

"Are you still trying to convince me to trade in my GOP card?"

"Yes, sir, Mr. Hopesmell!"

"I tell you what, shave your armpits and your legs and I'll do it."

"Why must you toy with me? Womyn are not objects. I know you know that. You *do* know that, don't you?"

"All right, all right. Keep your hair and your body odor. I tell you what . . . Call back tomorrow and I'll let you know. I just have to consult my attorney before I decide."

"I don't have a criminal record."

"I'm sure you don't. Just go see an Ani DiFranco show or something, and call me tomorrow. Or, better yet, send an e-mail. Good-bye, Edith."

"Okay, dude. Think on it. You'd be the object of my undying gratification! Howard Dean in 2004!!!"

> But you know, it's not unusual for senators to change party. For example, last night Ted Kennedy went from a party at Bennigan's to a party at Houlihan's.
> —David Letterman, on Jim Jeffords leaving the Republican Party

> What distinguishes these two instances of humanitarian intervention isn't principle, but politics. Kosovo was Clark's war. Iraq is Bush's.
> —Jacob Weisberg

"Pray, Charlie. Pray, faithful listeners. Pray for the Mad Dog and for whichever institution of liberal blasphemy that accepts her."

"'Hopesmell' does crack me up . . . Anyway, next we've got Bob on line one. He thinks you'll remember him. He's the Dubya Hater from Massachusetts?"

"Yeah, like there aren't a lot of those up there. Robert, you should be proud of your home. Taxachusetts makes my list of top fifty states, you know."

"Yeah, yeah, yeah."

"Okay, champ. In the bond of all things red, white, and blue, hit me like Nomah hits the first pitch fastball!"

"I'd like to hit *you*, slimeball!"

"Ah, another pacifist liberal, I see."

"First, you use your show to oust a wicked good man like Gray Davis, and now you're usin' it to tell lies about King George. I mean, come on. Wake up and smell the cocaine! Kerry is gonna bring it home for us. Even Dukakis could beat Son o' Bush!"

"Do you have a question for me today, Bob? Anything other than your rah, rah, rhetoric?"

"Sure . . . Who do you think is gonna be our next prez? And if not Kerry, then can Ted Kennedy ever win it all? Go Pats!"

CLICK.

"Sure he could. Just like your Red Sox'll win the Series. You *know* that every day is Halloween when you mention Kennedy and the presidency in the same sentence. All those 'wicked' scary skeletons just come dancing right out!"

"Seriously, TK's closet needs more cleaning out than Eminem's. His past really does make it a nonissue. I wasn't there at Chappaquiddick, but I have had a few beverages with the good senator. Yes, faithful listeners, despite my political leanings and his political shortcomings, that liberal and this conservative have shared some bar space. And let me tell you, TK makes Dean Martin look like a teetotaler. Besides, he's had the opportunity to run for president in the past and begged off all but once, soooo. Now, back to your original point . . .

"Who do I think will be our *next* president? Any attorney worth his retainer knows that you've asked me a leading question. An incumbent cannot, by the physics of grammar, be considered a 'next.' And Bush *will* win a second term in office. Continuing on that note, anyone with an ounce of common sense knows that I'm not a slimeball, Bob. Kerry the Ketchup Kid is. *Dr.* Dean is. Wesley 'Kosovo is Cool but Iraq is Whack' Clark is. Hillary *Rodman* Clinton is. But G. David Hopewell is not!"

"Tell it like it is, boss."

"I'm feeling it, Charlie. That Masshole got me hot! You knooooow that, by definition, part of being slimy is being deceitful. And what, if not deceitful, has Generalissimo Clark been? If anybody is going to have sympathy for the troops, it should be a former military man. But does he show any sympathy? Any compassion? An ounce of solidarity? No. He turns his back on the 'Army! Navy! Air Force! Marines! What a great place, it's a greeeeeeeat place . . . to start!!!' Love that song. Anyway, he wants to be the president, so what's he do? He turns his back on his former employer. Your typical Democrat, out for personal gain and willing to be as spotty as TK's driving record to get it. A real wolf in sheep's clothing. A military man in argyle sweaters. Hoo fa! And that, Bob from Liberalchusetts, is what I call slimy.

"Charlie, can you imagine being a soldier and knowing that a turncoat like Clark is your Commander-in-Chief?"

"That would be like the Sox hiring Roger Clemens back to manage."

"Or Gray Davis teaching a course on fiscal responsibility! Or on energy trading and risk management!"

"Exactly. And now, G., a word from our sponsors . . ."

Newsweek magazine says he's in the mountains of western Pakistan. And I guess if *Newsweek* could find him there, we could, too, if we wanted to.
—Wesley Clark, practicing a little Bush bashing while on the campaign trail

Realignment is a sudden transformation
that turns out to be permanent.
—Walter Dean Burnham

Chapter Twelve

America's Longest-Running Joke:
Still Running

Experience is not always the kindest
of teachers, but it is surely the best.
—Spanish proverb

121

The new millennium meant the end of Y2K mania, but it also meant the bursting of the economic bubble. Like many Americans, Al Gore suddenly found himself unemployed. Unlike most Americans, he had nobody else to blame.

Allowing Ralph Nader to take liberal votes was more costly than any hanky-panky taking place with Florida's Depends–wearing Democrats. Standing stiff as a cardboard cutout didn't do much to invigorate the college kids, either. Young Democrats saw a stick in the mud whose idea of fun was locking the lockbox and making out with his censorious wife on TV. Gore had Clinton's coattails to ride, but somewhere along the way, he fell off.

Admittedly, those coattails were a bit tattered and torn, and the decline in Democrat support had intensified during the 1990s. In 1992, for example, the Republicans held just 176 seats in the House. In 2003, that number was 229. The GOP currently controls twenty-one state legislatures, which is almost three times as many as in 1992. There were only eighteen Republican governors before Steamboat Willie came to town. Now, there are twenty-seven. Anyone else see the writing on the wall? If only the donkey could read it.

"In Franklin Roosevelt's administration," writes Fred Barnes, the executive editor of *The Weekly Standard*, "49 percent of voters said they were Democrats. But that number has been dropping ever since, and now roughly 32 percent of voters say they are."

The fastest-growing segment of the U.S. population is Latin Americans, and we know which party they are starting to support in greater and greater numbers. (The donkey had better get comfortable with "*burro*" and quick. The stubbornness, the reluctance to change, has always been a problem in the past.)

The Democratic Party's most prominent candidates have theories as to what's wrong with their party, as well as what should be done about it.

When not shouting like a professional wrestler, Howard Dean says the Democratic Party has "lost its soul" and is out of touch with its "true fighting self."

If Howard Dean can't stand the heat in the Democratic kitchen, he's going to melt in a minute once the Republicans start going after him.
—Joe Lieberman, giving Howie a little taste of his tough love (no sheep's clothing here)

Dean is highly qualified to hold office in Washington, D.C. I'm just not sure that office should be oval. The District of Columbia is smaller than Vermont by thirty thousand people. The only thing to stop him from becoming mayor is another Marion Barry comeback . . .

Dick Gephardt is finally done after trying, once again, to go the blue-collar route. He says that Howard Dean is a "fair-weather friend of the American worker" and that "There is no room for the cynical politics of manufactured anger and false convictions." At one point, before dropping out of the 2004 race, a testimonial on his Web site stated that Gephardt ". . . is now the flavor of the month, and the media is talking about him as the one to watch!" That's some wacky trash talk.

Indicative of the Democratic pathos is this strange message, also on Gephardt's Web

---

[41] Ironic when religion stands in the way of being a conservative, isn't it?

Get to Know the Candidates Interlude

Joe Lieberman, a conservative through and through, says that his mates are "too liberal" and "too secular." Lieberman's Land Rover Liberal supporters are even further right than Clinton's DLC. I wonder what's keeping him from becoming a Republican, anyway? Discomfort with the Christian Right? [41]

Lieberman would switch, except that Connecticut only elects Democratic senators. He has such little respect for his current party that he freely associates it with drug abuse. When the 2004 candidates were asked about having used marijuana, Lieberman's reply was, "Well, you know, I have a reputation for giving unpopular answers at Democratic debates . . . I never used marijuana. Sorry!"

Sorry?

"Come on, Hadassah. We're late for dinner at the Ashcrofts'!"

Not only are we going to New Hampshire . . .
We're going to South Carolina and Oklahoma
and Arizona and North Dakota and New Mexico,
and we're going to California and Texas and
New York. And we're going to South Dakota
and Oregon and Washington and Michigan.
And then we're going to Washington, D.C., to take
back the White House! *Yaaaaaaaaaaaargh!!!!!!!*
—Howard Dean, rallying the troops after losing
the Iowa Caucus[42]

site: "The latest *National Journal* 'Democratic Insiders Poll' showed that 'Gephardt is solidifying his status as the leading threat to front-runner Howard Dean.'" Cluelessness abounds when being second fiddle, not to mention being the "flavor of the month," is worth highlighting.[43] These are good things? And they say the GOP is out of touch with today's lingo.

No one is more in touch with the vernacular than young people, and the Reverend Al might be on to something. He says that the donkey has definitely fallen out of touch with the true identity of the Democratic Party, and that he wants to add an "equal rights" amendment to the Constitution: equal rights for women, equal

I would participate
as a participant.
—Al Sharpton on how
he would participate
(as part of a coalition
force in Iraq)

---

[42] That was no fireside chat. More like bonfire rhetoric.

[43] Second fiddle should have gone out with the original Electoral College.

124

> I think that a lot of it is that the Democratic Party has, in my judgment, not really focused on developing the next generation of leadership.
> —Al Sharpton, on *Hardball with Chris Matthews*

rights to education, and equal rights to health care. All three would qualify as "human rights." To his credit, while Sharpton has trimmed his waistline—trading in his sweat suits for some real suits, blue-collar à la John Edwards—he has widened his scope to include foreign affairs; but given the poor track record of Democrats far more experienced than he, there isn't much reason for optimism abroad. Guns and butter . . .

Sharpton doesn't really want to be president, anyway. He's interested in more gigs on *Saturday Night Live*, more of the limelight, a better seat at Rao's and Jimmy's, more press conferences in exotic locations like Puerto Rico, and doing the Detention Center Diet again.

John Kerry is a little too busy poofing up his hair in the Traficant-Van Buren tradition, and a little too busy being ticked off about everything and everyone, to comment on the status of the party. He's mad at Howard Dean for successfully flip-flopping on the war in Iraq, and he's mad about the polls. He's mad about just about everything.

> The civil rights arena is controlled by lawyers, with the winners and losers determined by rules most Americans neither understand nor are sympathetic with . . . There exists a reality of reverse discrimination that actually engenders racism.
> —John Kerry

> Democrats too often act like rural America is just someplace to fly over between a fund-raiser in Manhattan and a fund-raiser in Beverly Hills.
> —John Edwards

If I were married to the Heinz Ketchup lady, I'd probably be a bit happier (I'd probably have that convertible by now!). But not Kerry. He elucidated his concerns in a 2003 interview with *Rolling Stone*.

"I voted for what I thought was best for the country. Did I expect Howard Dean to go off to the left and say, 'I'm against everything?' Sure. Did I expect George Bush to fuck it up as badly as he did? I don't think anybody did." Sounds like somebody regrets lending his support to the war in Iraq. Loosen up, John. We're winning. Hussein has been captured. Your mama is a Forbes, you're knee-deep in condiments, and people from Massachusetts to Iowa dig your 'do. Speaking of which, maybe a more balanced diet would help level off your mood. Try mixing in a little Gulden's mustard every now and again.

Last but not least is the other John, the dark-horse John, John Edwards. The way Edwards sees it, the V word is where it's at: forget the left and right; the people will vote for the candidate who shares their values. VALUES! VALUES!! VALUES!!! More overused than "hero" is this word. A Jeep is now *heroic* and a bank has *values*, rather than just plain old value. Pure donkey doo!

> On the campaign trail, Edwards will mention—every five minutes or so—that his father worked in a textile mill and his mother retired from the post office.
> —David Brooks

And who, exactly, is Edwards trying to appeal to? Who is he hoping to make his constituency with all this talk of values? Homosexuals don't want to hear the V word. To them, it equates to no marriage license and no health insurance. Liberal intellectuals don't want to hear the V word, either. To them, it means shut the hell up during times of war and WTO meetings. And impoverished minorities certainly don't want to hear the V word, because it sounds like more of their men on death row. Ah, must be all those Southern textile-mill Catholics he's trying to woo. Doo!

In his *New York Times* article, "Forget the South," Ryan Lizza writes that, "Since 1964, the only Democrats elected president have been Southerners, and conventional wisdom holds that only a Democrat with a Southern base can win the presidency." Unfortunately for Edwards, Lizza's thesis—based on the electoral votes that Gore received in 2000—is that the South is no longer vitally important, and that Democrats should concentrate on New England. Good news for Kerry and Dean . . .

And lest I forget, there's one last Democrat worth mentioning. He's latecomer Wesley Clark. He would have an opinion on the state of the Democrats—if he could just remember that he's one of them. Like

The fact that Wesley Clark is going to testify in the middle of the primaries is fairly amazing. Clark is gambling that this will give him national and international press attention just at the time he needs it for the primaries. It will enable him to look very patriotic, very presidential.

—Michael Scharf on Clark's testimony at the Slobodan Milosevic trial

> I can walk the walk,
> not just talk the talk.
> —Wesley Clark,
> after neither walking
> nor talking in the
> 2004 Iowa Caucus

kids trading Animal Cards, the Republicans got Colin Powell and Clarence Thomas. The Democrats got Vermont's James Jeffords, the wacky, pro-Daschle independent, as well as General "Kosovo is Cool but Iraq is Whack" Clark.

After bursting onto the scene, though, his four stars quickly faded. Having an actual war hero on the team could only excite the Democrats for so long, and then it was back to the whining: more butter, less guns.

Thinking on this collection of close-but-no-cigarers, it's no wonder the donkey feels lost. How can he not worry about his party's leadership and his chances for a return to the Rose Garden? It's not just about the presidency, see. The Democrats can't afford to be the minority in the House and Senate again. Add in all of the aging jackasses set to retire, and suddenly the Love Boat is taking on water.

In the jaundiced glow of the arch, the donkey sees a magazine lying by the side of the road. The cover blows with each passing car, showing him a collection of eight familiar, smiling faces. The Democratic candidates from 2004 are all pictured.

The donkey would pick it up and read it, but there's that opposable thumb thing. Plus, in an asinine effort to build his self-esteem, his teachers had simply passed him on from one grade to the next. Knowing that he was an illegitimate child, they let him graduate even though he'd

> Hope is a bad thing. It means that you
> are not what you want to be. It means that
> part of you is dead, if not all of you. It means
> that you entertain illusions.
> —Henry Miller

never learned how to read. The illiterate donkey shuffles on, leaving the magazine and all those smiling hopefuls in the mud. Something may come of one of them. You never know . . . Right? Right! The donkey lets the light fill him with optimism; it glows so bright at this point that the arch seems to have doubled. He pauses before stepping onto the pavement, feeling just how full of hope he is. The return of blind hope, stubborn as the day is long.

> An election is coming. Universal peace is declared and the foxes have a sincere interest in prolonging the lives of the poultry.
> —T. S. Eliot

---

44 Daschle has only ever worked as a public servant; those are our tax dollars he's spending on his casa grande!

The Love Boat Interlude

Captain Steubing, played ably by Tom Daschle, stands at the helm of his sinking ship. All around him, staffers bail water. Rather than going down with the ship, he hops into a helicopter and flies home to South Dakota to testify on behalf of Republican Bill Janklow. Before returning to his troubled vessel, he stops off to see how construction is going on his new, $2 million D.C. mansion.[44] Shouldn't he live in South Dakota? Maybe go home when Congress isn't in session and check up on his constituents? Speaking of checking up, Gopher is struggling with Hillary's life vest, and Julie McCoy is bailing water with James Carville. Ted Kennedy is trying to get Isaac to fix him a drink, while Robert Byrd shouts "Bingo!" to no one in particular. Vicki is helping Doc to revive Jesse Jackson, but it doesn't seem to be working. The Democrats are going down.

129

Chapter Thirteen

Commonsense Radio Network:
Friday

You know, even the Democrats go too far
sometimes on downsizing government. One of
them said we ought to turn the Pentagon
into a triangle. And I said no, I am going to hold
the line with a veto threat for a rhombus!
—Bill Clinton

"Good morning, everybooooody! Respecting the rights of all American
citizens and convinced that the cream always rises to the top, this is
G. David Hopewell, and you're listening to Radio America! As we do
every day from 6:00 to 10:00 A.M., I'm coming to you live from the
studios of the Commonsense Radio Network, where the reception's
clear and so's the logic. Happy Friday, y'all!

"Well, as some of you already know, regular caller Edith 'Mad Dog' Qznicky asked me to write her a college recommendation yesterday, and we are awaiting her call. Until that time, I will not reveal my answer. Add a little drama to the show, right, Charlie?"

"Right, G. Man."

"And on that topic, Wayne from Iowa City called before. He's offered to not only write Mad Dog a recommendation, but to marry her once she turns twenty-one and converts to Klingon. How 'bout that, Charlie?"

"Love is in the air. And actually, Mad Dog did use our Instant Access late last night, so I've got an e-mail here. It sounds like she's still trying to get you to switch teams."

"Hand it over and I'll share with the people what our little Angry Puppy wrote . . . Well, faithful listeners, according to Mad Dog's *Webster's Dictionary*, a Democrat is, 'A person who believes in and practices the principle of equality of rights, opportunity, and treatment.' Ahhhh, very PC, but also very untempting and very untrue. Mad Dog ought to put the dictionary down and read some of her history books.

"I'll tell you what a Democrat is, Charlie . . . A Democrat is a Republican in a cheap suit. They're all closet conservatives. It's just that something's missing from their lives, and rather than go out and get it, rather than go out and make good, they choose to join up with everybody else who's missing out, and I guess the shared whining makes them feel better. Just like listening to my show makes them feel better, for *some* reason.

"A Democrat is a Republican with low self-esteem and even lower earning potential; a Republican with bad skin, bad judgment, and bad credit. How do you like that, Mad Dog? I've changed my mind. No recommendation for you!"

"While you're reading from our Instant Access, G., we have a pretty funny e-mail here titled 'You've Gotta Believe.' I think you'll like it better than that definition."

"Thanks, Charlie . . . Okay, in order to be a Democrat, 'you've gotta believe that businesses create oppression and that governments create prosperity.' Right on! 'You've gotta believe that guns, in the hands of law-abiding Americans, are more of a threat than U.S. nuclear weapon technology in the hands of the Chinese. You've gotta believe that there was no art before federal funding, and that AIDS is spread by a lack of federal funding; that global temperatures are less affected by cyclical changes in the earth's climate and more affected by yuppies driving SUVs.' Yep, Lieberman and all those Land Rover Liberals . . . 'That building someone's self-esteem is more important than having them earn it; that the military, not corrupt politicians, starts wars; that taxes are too low, but ATM fees are too high; that standardized tests are racist, but quotas and affirmative action are not; that Hillary is a lady and Bill is a gentleman; that the only reason socialism hasn't worked anywhere is because the right people haven't been in charge; that illegal Democratic party funding by the Chinese is in the best interest of the U.S.; and finally, that Republicans telling the truth belong in jail, but a liar and sex offender belongs in the White House.'"

"Well said."

"And well read!"

"The hits just keep coming this morning, G. Man."

"Is it a call from Mad Dog?"

"No. Continuing with the Instant Access, we just got something that actually qualifies as news. Jon from Connecticut reports that the first-ever incident of donkey road kill has taken place. I guess an old jackass was hit while trying to cross I-95. A witness said that it looked like the animal was trying to get to McDonald's. Can you believe this?"

"After ten years on the air, Charlie, I believe just about everything."

> Too nice is neighbor's fool.
> —Dutch proverb

133

"The report is that the donkey was making a beeline for the takeout window when he was struck by a guy in an old convertible."

"Wham, bam, see ya Sam! Hey, why'd the donkey cross the road? To get jacked! Ha, ha! What a story. Thank you, Jon from Connecticut. You've made my morning!"

"Not an ounce of sorrow, G. Man? Aren't you an animal lover?"

"Of course, Charlie, but it's just such a fitting end for the donkey. It's so fitting, in fact, that I change my mind. I will write that recommendation for Mad Dog. Because with education comes common sense, and because the world is a better place with more common sense and less false ideology. Between me and Conspiracy Theory Wayne, we'll send Mad Dog off to college—if anything, so that she doesn't end up like that stupid donkey. For far too long, the Democrats have left their constituents in the rearview mirror like so much political roadkill. But back to college and Ms. Qznicky; I promise you, Mad Dog, you won't end up a sheep in wolf's clothing nor a wolf in sheep's clothing nor a limp and lifeless jackass. I won't allow it!"

"That's awfully nice of you, boss."

"Hey, I'm a nice guy when I want to be."

"Aren't we all?"

"I wish that were true, Charles. I really do."

In a nation of malls and fast food,
regionalism still counts in politics.
—Todd S. Purdum

One inherent characteristic of the party
still holds true from Lincoln to Bush II:
Republicans have never liked Democrats.
And that is a trend that will
undoubtedly continue.
—Douglas Brinkley,
in a review of Lewis L. Gould's
Grand Old Party

A man who moralises is usually a hypocrite, and a woman who moralises is invariably plain.
—Oscar Wilde

Talk that does not end in any kind of action is better suppressed altogether.
—Thomas Carlyle

'76 Cadillac Convertible

For a younger person it is almost a sin to be too much occupied with himself; but for the aging person it is a duty and a necessity to give serious attention to himself. After having lavished its light upon the world, the sun withdraws its rays in order to illumine itself.

—Carl Jung, from *Modern Man in Search of a Soul*

So, I may be an average joe that nobody knows, but every now and again I make a difference. I teach somebody's kid about the Bill of Rights or show him how to organize his three-ring binder, his book bag, his life. I make a difference at the polls every now and again, too, turning 50 percent into 51 percent. And as expected, whoever appeals to me most gets my 1 percent. My vote. To the victor goes the spoils.

I hate the Democratic Party because it started so optimistically and is carrying on so poorly—just like the old donkey; farts so weak they die in the wind. Modern-day Democrats aren't worth the wasted ground they make their mascot feed from.[45] These so-called leaders, men like Bill and women like Hillary, would surely incite Burr-like rage in the patriarch of the party. But the political machine that Thomas Jefferson once fired up like a John Deere has sputtered with neglect. No one's replaced the spark plugs, and the filters are as clogged as the gas line. The blades have gone dull and the headlights were kicked out long ago. The Democratic Party is no '69 Corvette. At this point, it isn't even a rusted-out '76 Eldorado.

Jefferson would shudder to think of a McDonald's. It represents everything he feared and everything Hamilton embraced: the homogenizing of America; the nullification of the individuality of the states in lieu of fast-food federalism. Corvette, Cadillac, and John Deere, suddenly all one and the same. No way to tell the difference between tractors and convertibles, hawks and doves, sheep and wolves.[46]

Moving away from the magazine, the donkey continues his trek down Memory Lane. He recalls making Jefferson laugh as he dropped those road apples for Hamilton to step in. But just as his flatulence has turned worthless and weak, so has his party. It has become the Federalist Party: big government that panders to the wealthy and

---

[45] Forcing the poor fellow to consider carnivorous ways, risking life and limb just to get some McDonald's. Pitiful.

[46] The donkey and the elephant?!?!

forces the states to play second fiddle to the Washington bureaucracy.[47] This is what embarrasses the old donkey most. Shame is the most misguided of motivators.

As he steps across the white line, he can see the drive-through window. It all makes sense now; those mythic, glowing arches. Not The Gateway Arch in St. Louis, but the Golden Arches. This is that fabled mecca of poor health: McDonald's, Mickey D's, Casa de Cholesterol! No better time than the present to throw caution to the wind, he decides. No better time to submit to his urges. No one is paying him any mind, anyway. Certainly none of those he used to preach to, holier than thou, about eating healthy. The donkey's heart swells with deserving, like Hart with his Rice and Truman with his deep freezers. After a lifetime of Bermuda grass, he isn't ashamed to say that he *deserves* a cheeseburger. Some fries, too. He rationalizes that this is, after all, the cuisine of his constituency: the average joe. With each bite, he will come closer and closer to finally being one with the people. There might even be a reporter around to snap some photos . . .

The donkey is sucked back from his reverie as the drive-through cashier calls his name. "Burro! Burro!!!"[48]

Her warning is interpreted as an invitation and he brays with excitement, sure now that you *can* have your Happy Meal and eat it, too.

The donkey's hooves click reassuringly. The decision to give McDonald's a try makes him feel like the days of twenty-loss seasons are behind him now. He can't wait to order a burger, fries, and a Coke. Well, maybe a Diet Coke.

139

---

[47] James H. Boren writes, "Guidelines for bureaucrats: 1) When in charge, ponder. 2) When in trouble, delegate. 3) When in doubt, mumble."

[48] The Hispanic vote really is more important than that Pancho Villa promise. And his grumbling stomach really is more important than his photo op ideals.

As close as he is now, even the donkey can see what the two arches represent: self-interest and philanthropy. He's done with choosing the former and trying to sell it as the latter. The only choice he cares about now is Big Mac or Quarter Pounder. As fierce as a presidential debate, he weighs the pros and cons of special sauce, lettuce, cheese.

The donkey is so consumed with his Big Mac meditations that he forgets to look left as he steps out onto the highway. He never does see the convertible coming his way, the driver smiling like it was a vintage 'Vette and not a corroded old Caddy. The donkey never does learn what *"¡Pare!"* means. Nor *"¡Cuidado!"*
CLICK!

Bibliography

The Columbia Encyclopedia: Sixth Edition. Edited by Paul Lagassé. New York: Columbia University Press, 2003.

The Dictionary of Cultural Literacy. Edited by E. D. Hirsch Jr., Joseph F. Kett, and James Trefil. Boston: Houghton Mifflin Company, 1991.

The International Dictionary of Thoughts. Compiled by John P. Bradley, Leo F. Daniels, and Thomas C. Jones. Chicago: J. G. Ferguson Publishing Company, 1969.

The New Dictionary of Thoughts. Compiled by Tryon Edwards. New York: StanBook Incorporated, 1977.

The Quotable Politician. Edited by William B. Whitman. Guilford, Connecticut: The Lyons Press, 2003.

www.slate.com

Toole, John Kennedy. *The Confederacy of Dunces.* New York: Grove Press, 1980.

Uncle John's Giant 10th Anniversary Bathroom Reader. Ashland, Oregon: Bathroom Readers' Press, 1997.

Webster's New World Dictionary of American English: Third College Edition. Edited by Victoria Neufeldt. Cleveland and New York: Webster's New World, 1988.

Witcover, Jules. *Party of the People: A History of the Democrats.* New York: Random House, 2003.

Zinn, Howard. *A People's History of the United States: 1492–Present.* New York: Perennial Classics, 2001.

Acknowledgments

My gratitude to George Donahue. It's nice when an editor need not be acknowledged with a concession speech!

My thanks to Chuck Howe for his insights, to Mike Olsen and Eric Hinz for their persuasive exaggerations, and to Sergio Quijano for serving the best mojítos this side of Havana.

And finally, all the hugs in the world to Alicia and Noelle Solís. You are the epitome of hate's opposite.

142

About the Author

Randy Howe is a registered Independent who chooses his poker and golf buddies by how qualified they are and not according to political affiliation. He lives in Connecticut with his conservative wife and liberal daughter, a cat that could care less, and a dog that will vote for whomever leaves the lid off the trash. He is the author of *Flags of the Fifty States and Their Incredible Histories* and *The Quotable Teacher*, as well as—in a gracious nod to impartiality—*Why I Hate the Republicans*.

In order to become the
master, the politician
poses as the servant.
—Charles de Gaulle,
French prime minister

It's looking increasingly
as if Democrats will be
the party of anger in
2004. Republicans may
as well be the party of
reform and hope.
—David Brooks,
in *The New York Times*